Stock and Forex

2 BOOKS IN 1

Stock market investing for beginners

Forex for beginners

Gualtiero Favole

Table of Contents 1

Table of Contents 2

Stock Market Investing for Beginners

The Ultimate Guide to Creating a Profitable Portfolio

Gualtiero Favole

Introduction

Welcome to "*Stock Market Investing for Beginners. The Ultimate Guide to Creating a Profitable Portfolio.*" This is the beginning of an exciting journey that will lead you to become financially independent. In the following pages, you will uncover the secrets the stock traders and financial experts know but don't want to share with you. Herein, you'll find a treasure trove of insider secrets. If you believe there is a magic formula for making money investing in stock, you'll find that all it takes is the right know-how.

Throughout this book, we will discuss the information you need to know. We will dispense with the fluff and focus on the meat and potatoes. You will get the real information on how to make money, thereby creating a solid financial life for you and your family.

We are going to delve into the secrets of day trading. If you are keen on rolling up your sleeves, day trading is the right approach for you. You'll find out how you can make money day trading, from the comfort of your home and office, and without having to work more than you already do.

We are also going to look into swing trading. This trading approach is highly profitable. However, you need to know when to strike. In doing so, you'll be able to cash in on market opportunities that don't come around very often. But when they do, you will be ready for them.

We are going to discuss position trading. This is a long-term trading strategy that will allow you to maximize your returns. This is where you hit home runs. They take time to set up. But once you have the right deal in place, it can be very rewarding for you. As such, position trading is the ultimate approach for high-value investors.

If this sounds too good to be true, then stick around to learn how you can make the most of your time and effort. You are surely interested in investing as you are looking for the best way to help your family be financially secure.

You can't guarantee your family's financial wellbeing by taking on another job. Nor can you become financially independent by working longer hours. This is the reason why stock investing is so appealing. Plenty of other folks out there have made stock investing work for them. Now, it's your turn to make some real money.

Ultimately, you can continue to live your usual life knowing that you have all of your bases covered. You can afford to continue your day job, not because you have to, but because you want. This is the type of freedom that can come from stock market investing.

The secrets are here.

Once you see them in action, you will realize that it's simple to achieve. However, the right know-how is essential to making things work for you. So, buckle up because we are going to cover a lot of information. Rest assured that the information we will discuss is presented in a clear and concise form.

Thanks again for choosing this book, make sure to leave a short review on Amazon if you enjoy it, i'd really love to hear your thoughts!

Let' get down to business!

Chapter 1: Why Should You Invest?

To invest, or not invest? That is the question.

When you think about investing, what comes to mind?

For most people, the idea of investing is very similar to gambling. They roll the dice on a stock, win big, and solve all of their problems. However, this is something seen in the movies but not in real life. In real life, investing is a carefully planned action. By taking the time to carefully plan investments, returns are often much greater than expected.

Therefore, investing is something that we need to see as an opportunity. If you look at investing as pain today, fun tomorrow, then you will never make it. When you commit to investing because you know you will achieve your objectives, then you are well on your way to making some serious cash.

So, let's take a look at the reason why you should invest.

Make Extra Income

The majority of folks that invest do so to supplement their current income. It's hard to make a decent living from just one income stream. Moreover, it's hard to make money by working longer hours. Therefore, most people look for other means of supplementing their monthly income.

This is where investing comes into play.

When you invest money, you eventually get paid returns on your investments. Typical investment vehicles such as mutual and index funds pay interest on a monthly or quarterly basis. They provide additional funds that can be put toward any number of purposes. However, the returns you can get from these investments are often underwhelming.

Many times, the returns you get from mutual funds can be disappointing. This is the reason why lots of people look toward investing directly into stocks. By cutting out middlemen, investors stand to make far better gains. As such, savvy, proactive investors use day, swing, and position trading as a way of generating regular income. When you come to combine your regular income plus income from investing, you have a winning formula that can help you fund a comfortable lifestyle.

Planning for Retirement

This is a long-term approach. Investment accounts such as IRAs and 401(k)s provide a way of financing expenses during retirement years. These investments work very well for folks who have time to spare. Thus, the younger you get started, the more money you stand to make. By the same token, the longer you take to open one of these accounts, the less time you have to fund your retirement.

Therefore, investing in stocks makes sense for those looking to save up for retirement. Depending on your strategy, you can simply roll over investment to make your nest egg grow. Over time, you'll not only have a regular income but also a substantial amount of capital racked up. As a result, stock investing makes perfect sense for those saving up for retirement.

Earn Passive Income

Passive income is one of the most intriguing reasons to invest. Passive income basically means you don't actively work for the income you earn. This may sound too good to be true, but it is a fact. When you invest in stocks, you can set up your trading system to do the work for you. Nowadays, virtually all trading is done through computers. There is algorithmic trading you can use to help you automate all of your transactions. Consequently, all you need to do is set up your trades and let the system handle the rest.

By taking advantage of automated trading, you can devote a couple of hours a day, or a week even, to your trades. Once you have everything set up, you can sit back and watch the action. Of course, you need to stay on top of the action. But doing so won't require you to spend hours in front of the computer.

Also, there are folks who choose to make trading a full-time job. If you choose to do so, you can work both actively and passively. You can set up trades to work automatically while you focus on other directly. In a way, you are conducting multiple trades at once.

If you have ever wondered how stockbrokers make so much money in a short time frame, this is the answer. They use the power of automated trading to do multiple transactions at once.

Achieve Financial Independence

Financial independence means that you don't need to work to finance your lifestyle. In other words, you choose to work. You work because you want to, not because you have to. This is the true meaning of freedom. Additionally, this is not something that you can achieve by working a job.

People who become financially independent achieve this by investing in stocks, real estate, or business ventures. They reach a point where they have regular income without actively working. Therefore, they don't need to work a 9 to 5 routine to make money. They have an automated system that works for them.

When you achieve financial independence, you can afford to make time for the things you have always wanted. You can provide for your loved ones without having to sacrifice your time. You can prioritize your health rather than work. In the end, financial independence is the ultimate goal most people seek.

The truth is that most people say they want to be rich. What they mean is that they don't want to worry about paying the bills every month. What most people really want is to have a comfortable life in which they can afford to do whatever they want, whenever they want. Thus, they are not obsessed with a specific amount of money in their bank account.

Now, if you are keen on becoming truly wealthy, then you can certainly achieve this through stock investing. It takes time and patience, but it pays off in the end. The principles in this book will help you get there. But you need to start investing today. The longer you wait, the longer it will take you to get to the promised land.

Chapter 2: Fundamentals of Stock Market Investing

To be successful in the stock market, you need to understand the nuts and bolts that hold it together. Generally speaking, the stock market functions like any other market. There are buyers and sellers that come together to agree on a price. As such, price is the ultimate mechanism by which investors can carry out transactions.

So, let's discuss how the market prices stocks.

How to Price Stocks

The core element of pricing stocks is supply and demand. In short, when there is high demand (lots of buyers) and low supply (few sellers), then price goes up. In contrast, when there is low demand (few sellers) and high supply (lots of sellers), price goes down. If sellers and buyers are equal, then there is a perfect market price. This is the general rule that's applied to all commodities in a free market. Unless a market is manipulated, supply and demand will determine the bulk of price action.

However, there are additional factors that determine pricing in financial markets. The main factor is psychological. By "psychological" we mean what investors believe may or may not happen. For instance, if investors feel that a specific company is undervalued, they will flock to buy it up. As such, their desire to own this company's stock will cause the price to go up. By the same token, if investors feel there is something wrong with a company, its stock price will plummet.

Also, economic conditions may lead investors to think twice about buying and/or selling. For example, during a recession, investors may be far more cautious. After all, they might be concerned about the long-term effects of the current economic outlook.

Furthermore, company financials, management, and competition play a significant role in its stock valuation. If a company has solid financials, reputable management, and is at the top of its industry, then you have a winner. However, don't be surprised to hear an investor bet on long shots. These are companies that are unproven, or might be poised for a turnaround after a tough spell. However, always be careful with betting on long shots. There is never any guarantee they will play out.

Looking to the Future

To look into the future, you need to look into the past. With stock prices, you can glean into the future by looking at the history of price action. Individual companies all have historical data on the behavior of its market valuation. This information allows you to look toward the future. From its past trend, you can figure out what might happen. Of course, nothing is certain. Still, you may be able to get a good picture of the future.

Therefore, you must become familiar with charts and graphs. These elements are the graphic representation of the data pertaining to price action. The most common graph is a line graph. Line graphs are perfect at showing the behavior of a stock's trend. Moreover, it will enable you to get a sense of what will happen by its patterns.

The study of quantitative data is called "technical analysis." Technical analysis is crucial to making informed decisions. If you make investment decisions based on your subjective appreciation, then you are basically guessing. As such, you must have objective data to make reasonable assumptions on a stock. Otherwise, the risk of losing on a deal grows exponentially.

Market Organization

When you hear about the "stock market," what you are really hearing about is the collection of stock exchanges located throughout the world. A stock exchange is a physical location in which buyers and sellers of financial assets come together. The most famous stock exchange in the world is the New York Stock Exchange located on Wall Street in New York City. This is the place where the bulk of the transactions happen in the United States. Nevertheless, there are similar exchanges in Philadelphia, Chicago, and Miami.

Additionally, there are a number of stock exchanges around the world. Some of the largest are located in European cities such as London, Paris, Frankfurt, and Madrid. In Asia, the most predominant stock exchanges can be found in Shanghai, Tokyo, and Seoul. There are other markets in Latin America, as well.

When you buy and sell stocks, among other assets, you trade directly in one of these stock exchanges. As a result, you must become familiar with the various kinds of assets trade in them. Please keep in mind that you won't always find the same assets in all markets. Some markets specialize in one type of asset over another. Moreover, companies are listed on a single exchange. Thus, a company that is listed in the United States cannot be listed in another country. So, if you are keen on trading specific companies, you might have to look at an overseas market, as well.

Asset Classes

Stocks are not the only assets that are traded in financial markets. There are a plethora of assets to choose from. In this book, we're focusing on stocks. Nevertheless, here is a list of the assets you can trade in financial markets:

- Government bonds (both US and other countries)

- Commodities (agricultural products, cattle, precious metals, industrial metals, energy)

- Currencies (any currency in the world)

- Derivatives (futures, swaps, options)

- Funds (mutual, index, exchange-traded)

These asset classes have a number of instruments you can buy and sell. Some are great for a "buy and hold" strategy, like bonds, while others are better for short-term investments such as commodities. Ultimately, you can choose to invest in any of these asset classes based on your expectations and your goals.

We recommend starting out with stock. It is the best way to get started before branching out into other asset classes. Since some transactions require a greater amount of experience and study, it is important to master stock trading before taking the plunge into other asset classes. Still, you can build a diversified portfolio by investing in various asset classes. Diversification is a great strategy especially when you are looking to protect yourself against long-term risk.

Chapter 3: How to Create an Investment Timeline

Creating an investment timeline is all about managing your expectations. When you are keenly aware of the potential in the market, it is easy to get caught up in the excitement. Many investors engage in wishful thinking. They believe they can score a huge deal that will solve all of their problems.

This is something that you'd only see in the movies.

While it is possible to knock one out of the park, doing so requires time and research. If you can spot a deal like this, you might be poised to clean up. Otherwise, you may find yourself searching for the elusive "big one."

Managing Expectations

The most important part of managing expectations is being realistic. By "realistic" we mean understanding that it takes time to build a winning strategy. Therefore, you need to have patience in the early going. For instance, a realistic assumption would be to make a few hundred dollars in your first month of trading. It may not be enough to pay for all of your expenses, but it would be a welcome windfall.

It is practically impossible to indicate a specific sum of money you could make in your first few weeks of trading. Depending on your strategy and starting capital, you could make anywhere from $200 to $300, to several thousand. However, it's also important to keep in mind that most investors lose money at first. By sticking to their game plan, they turn things around and make up lost ground.

Based on this, it is reasonable to assume that you will make enough money to supplement your monthly income in the early going. If you start with an investment capital such as a few hundred dollars, you might be able to turn that into $100 or more.

Here is a reasonable way of determining how much you could make based on your starting capital. Average market returns range between 5% to 10% annually. If you break it down, that's roughly 1% to 2% a month. That might not seem like a lot. But when you multiply it over the number of transactions and investment capital, you could potentially make a fair amount of money. Later on, we'll discuss the strategies that you can use to maximize your returns.

Most investors reach complete financial independence at different points in their lives. The easy answer is this: the simpler your lifestyle, the sooner you can become financially independent. Consequently, if you only need $1,500 a month to finance your lifestyle, you may get there in a couple of years, if not much sooner. In contrast, if you need $5,000 a month to fund your living expenses, then it might take you several years to get there. In the end, it all boils down to your overall lifestyle.

Determine the Lifestyle You Want

Speaking of lifestyles, having a clear idea of what your ideal lifestyle is, constitutes the backbone of your investment timeline. There is nothing wrong with dreaming big. However, it's important for you to know that financial independence is about financing your lifestyle without the need to work for an indefinite time frame. For some, "indefinite" might mean the rest of their lives. For others, it might just mean taking off as much time as they want.

To calculate how much money you need to finance your lifestyle, all you need is to crunch the numbers. Take your current lifestyle. Use it as a baseline. Add up all of your expenses in a month. Try your best to include everything you spend on. The greater the detail, the more accurate the number.

Now, let's assume your monthly number is $1,000. Thus, you would need to produce an income of $1,000 per month to finance your lifestyle. This is your baseline.

The next step is to figure out the lifestyle that you want. To calculate this number, you would need to figure out how much it would cost you to finance this type of life. You would need to add up all the expenses that would be involved and then come up with a number. So, let's assume that your ideal lifestyle would cost you $2,000. Hence, you would need to first produce $1,000 to achieve financial independence, but then produce $2,000 to get to your ideal lifestyle.

Calculating Financial Independence

To calculate how long it will take you to be financially independent is about consistently hitting the number you need to finance your lifestyle. When you can consistently make enough money to finance your lifestyle, you know you're there. So, if you are able to produce $1,000 (according to our example) for three consecutive months, then you know you have hit the mark.

Let's assume a 5% monthly return rate on your investment. So, to produce $1,000 in profits, you would need to invest $20,000 each month. A 5% return on $20,000 is $1,000. If you have $20,000 on hand at the moment, then generating this type of return will take you a couple of months. But if you are starting out with $1,000, then it will take you several months to achieve this type of return.

To come up with a fairly accurate number, let's take a 5% return on $1,000. That's $50. Next, roll over your profits plus investment capital. So, in month number two, you would invest $1,050. At a 5% return, month number two would yield $52.50. On month number three, you would invest $1,102.50.

In this example, we're using small numbers and assuming very conservative returns. Nevertheless, it illustrates the type of calculation you would need to make to reach your desired target. The main thing to keep in mind here is to resist the temptation to take out your profits during the first few months. If you can simply keep rolling over your investments every month, you'll build up your investment capital. Before you know it, you'll have a large capital to work with. This will make reaching your desired target much easier.

Chapter 4: How to Define Your Investment Strategy

Having an investment strategy is a fundamental aspect of successful stock market trading. Without it, you're essentially groping in the dark. While you may be very adept at technical analysis, you will find it hard to have a clear direction for your portfolio. Of course, you can still make money. However, you won't make the best return you could make.

It is important for you to determine what your game plan is going to be. When you have this plan worked out, you can then go about finding the stocks to match your aims. In this chapter, we are going to look at three great investment strategies you can use to make serious gains.

Buy and Hold

The "buy and hold" strategy is a long-term strategy. In this strategy, you buy up assets and hold on to them until their price shoots up. At that point, you can sell your holdings. Now, it should be noted that the definition of "long term" in stock trading is any time frame over a month. As such, you should expect to hold on to stocks for at least a month.

This strategy is great when you find undervalued stocks. For instance, companies that have great track records but have fallen on hard times. Oil companies are a great example of this. Oil companies have no fault in geopolitical issues that cause the price of oil to fall. Nevertheless, when the price of oil plummets, oil companies take serious hits.

To capitalize on this phenomenon, you buy up oil stocks when they sink. Then, you hold on to them until the price of oil rebounds. Thus, oil stocks rebound as well. In some cases, it might be a question of days. In other cases, it might be a question of weeks. Ultimately, you need to be on top of news and developments across various industries.

High-Frequency Trading

High-frequency trading, or HFT, is a staple of day traders. This is a very short-term strategy. It consists of making multiple trades over and over. You don't make a lot of money per trade with this strategy. However, when you multiply your gains over a large number of transactions, the profits add up.

To make this strategy work, you need to find a stock that is trading in a range. This means that they go up to a specific value and then back down to a certain value. Meanwhile, they don't typically deviate from these limits. As a result, you can fairly predict where the price action will be.

Many times, HFT traders make pennies per trade. But when the total number of trades is calculated, the results could add up to hundreds of dollars a day. Therefore, it is a good strategy to use while you execute the "buy and hold" with other stocks.

Also, HFT is great for investors who are starting with very little investment capital. As such, HFT traders move the same investment capital over and over again. For instance, the invest $1,000 over and over making profits on the same amount of money. In the end, they generate returns is if they had invested $100,000.

As a novice investor, you ought to consider HFT. It will require you to spend some time at your computer setting up deals. But once you get the hang of it, you can easily set everything up at the start of your day, and then sit back to take in all the action.

Value Investing

Value investing consists of finding undervalued stocks and holding them until they bounce back. Now, the main difference between value investing and the buy and hold strategy is that value investing looks to find companies that will rebound in a shorter time frame. In the case of the buy and hold, you are looking to hold stocks for over a month. In value investing, you're looking to hold stocks for days or a couple of weeks.

The trick to value investing is finding stocks that are poised to make a comeback sooner rather than later. To execute the value investing strategy, you need to look at a company's book value. The term "book value" refers to a company's share price based on its accounting. As such, a company's financials will tell you what their share price is really worth. Then, you must compare the company's book value with its market valuation. If you find that the company's market valuation is below its book value, then you have an undervalued company.

However, there is a catch.

When going about value investing, you must ensure that the company is not in serious trouble. Therefore, you need to do your homework carefully. In some cases, a company may be going through a temporary situation. This is not a reflection of poor management or bad financials. As such, you can assume the company will bounce back.

In value investing, things can happen very quickly. So, you need to be ready for the possible changes that may take place. Still, it is a very good strategy when you're looking for an intermediate step between the buy and hold and HFT.

Setting Objectives

The strategies mentioned in this chapter are all aligned to your objectives. Whether you're looking to supplement your monthly income or become a billionaire, you need to be clear on what you want to achieve. Then, you can align your strategy.

Generally speaking, novice investors start with HFT, then move up to value investing before using the buy and hold. Ultimately, you can combine all three strategies to keep your portfolio engaged in the short, medium, and long term. As such, you will gain exposure to all investment time frames.

This approach will help you make short-term gains while allowing you to cash in on the big trades that happen in the long term. This is the reason why it is so important for you to do your homework. Thus, the more informed you are, the easier it will be for you to make some serious returns.

Chapter 5: Fundamentals of Day Trading

To invest in stocks, you can go the usual route. So, you can buy mutual funds or pay a stockbroker to manage your portfolio. However, this route will only get you so far. You'll be quite surprised to find the potential returns to be quite underwhelming.

Because of underwhelming returns, many investors choose to go at it alone. This is the reason why they turn to day trading. In this chapter, we'll be looking at the fundamentals of day trading, and why it might be a good choice for you.

Definition of Day Trading

Day trading is a stock investing approach in which the investor takes full control of their portfolio. In other words, the investor decides what stocks to buy and sell. Moreover, the investor decides when to make trades happen.

By definition, day trading is a short-term trading approach. Investors open and close positions on the same trading day. Therefore, they start and end the day with a clean slate. The reason for this is simplicity. If you leave positions open overnight, you might become vulnerable to external factors. The result may be unexpected shifts in price action.

Therefore, investors seek to avoid becoming vulnerable by closing all of their positions at the end of the trading. As such, they cash out for the day. This is a highly practical approach as it enables investors to avoid dealing with possible price shocks that may occur at the start of the trading day.

Day trading is perfect for those investors who are starting out with relatively small investment capital and are looking to make short-term gains. For those investors with larger investment capital, day trading may be one part of their overall investment approach.

How to Get Started With Day Trading

To get started with day trading, you need a brokerage account. A brokerage account is an agreement that you enter with a financial institution. This institution is a duly license stock trading corporation. Hence, this corporation allows you to gain access to the market through the use of their trading platform. In short, you become a stockbroker yourself. The only downside is that you are solely responsible for anything that happens. So, if you lose all your money, you have no one to blame but yourself.

There are two main types of brokerage accounts. There is a "full service" account. This account type gives you all the bells and whistles. These accounts charge a sign-up fee in addition to transaction fees per trade. Yet, they provide you with real-time quotes and analytics. Also, they provide expert advice and recommendations. Thus, they facilitate the process of deciding where to allocate your funds.

The other type of account is a "discount" account. When you sign up with a discount broker, you mainly receive access to the trading platform but without the bells and whistles. Therefore, you need to figure out where you can get information on the stocks you wish to trade. The good thing about discount brokers is that they charge a one-time sign-up fee. They also have lower transaction fees per trade. Although, you would need to buy trade bundles as opposed to a pay-as-you-go strategy.

Once you sign up for a brokerage account, you are ready to trade. It is relatively straightforward. However, do keep in mind that brokerage accounts vary in conditions. Some may require you to have several thousand dollars' worth of investment capital while others may only require you to have as little as $500.

One very important thing to keep in mind is the free demo account. Any reputable brokerage firm will grant you free access to the platform via a demo account. In a demo account, you play the real game using monopoly money. As such, you are trading on the real platform, with real data and analytics, but not with real money. This is why a demo account is great. It allows you to test out your strategy before you go live with real trades. It affords you the opportunity to make mistakes without losing your shirt in the process.

The Best Day Trading Strategy

The best day trading strategy, especially for beginners, is HFT. HFT is quite easy to master. That is why HFT is the best strategy for new investors. Plus, it doesn't require a great deal of investment capital. If you sign up for a discount account, you can turn $500 into a fairly decent amount in a few weeks. Naturally, the more trades you make, the greater your chances of making your capital grow.

Early on, you ought to consider rolling over your profits. It is recommended that you resist the temptation of pulling out your winnings. The idea is to build up your investment capital so that it can produce even greater returns.

The only catch to HFT is transaction fees. Please make sure that you are perfectly aware of how much your broker charges per trade. It could be that high transaction fees zap your profits. To avoid getting hit with high transaction fees, it's a good idea to purchase bundles. For example, your broker may offer 10 trades for $2.99. This type of package allows you to calculate your cost, thereby enabling you to visualize your returns.

How to Determine if Day Trading Is for You

Naturally, day trading is not for everyone. To be successful, day trading requires a commitment to learning the trading platform. By learning the platform, you'll be able to set up all your deals appropriately. Then, you can let the platform do its job.

Day trading may not be right for you if you are looking to become a passive investor. As a passive investor, you are not keen on becoming actively involved in trading. Nevertheless, day trading can help you become a passive investor as it would only require you to go about setting up your deals at the outset of the trading day. By the end of the day, the system will close out your positions. Meanwhile, you can spend your time researching your next move.

Chapter 6: How to Succeed at Day Trading

When you go about day trading, it is essential to have strategies that you can use to help you make money most of the time. If you lack reliable go-to strategies, you may find yourself guessing about what to do. Thus, having a clear idea of what you can do at all times is the best way to get ahead in the game.

In this chapter, we are going to take a look at some core strategies to help you make money while also helping you get ahead of the game. Now, it's worth noting that most investors have a 50% to 60% success rate. In general, investors win most trades. However, please be prepared to lose. So, your strategy boils down to what you can do when things don't work out. Your reaction in these situations will enable you to become a highly successful investor.

Core Strategies

To be successful, you must follow these core strategies. They are cross-cutting recommendations that you can implement any time you choose to enter a trade. Moreover, these strategies are time-tested tactics that can keep you safe from the mistake novice investors make. Therefore, do keep them at the forefront of your mind as you engage in stock investing.

Money management

Money management refers to the way you manage your investment capital. This is an approach that you can use to help you develop discipline in your asset allocation. There are two main rules that you need to follow.

- **The golden rule**. This rule refers to limiting the amount of capital you sink into individual trades. The golden rule states that you must never invest more than 2% of your total investment capital into a single trade. While you can invest the full sum of your capital, you shouldn't invest it all in a single trade. Please keep in mind that the more money you sink into an individual trade, the greater the risk.

- **Doubling down**. When investors lose money, they are tempted to invest twice as much in the next trade to compensate for the loss in the previous one. This strategy is highly dangerous. It can lead you to lose twice as much as you did before. For example, if you lost $100 on a trade, you might be tempted to invest $200 in the one. However, if something goes wrong, you risk losing $200 on top of the original $100. So, it's best to simply follow your strategy. You'll eventually recoup your losses.

Timing the market

Generally speaking, the largest amount of trading activity happens at the beginning and end of the trading session. Therefore, these are the times when you need to jump into the fray. The first two hours of the trading day show a flurry of activity. Here, you can perfectly implement an HFT strategy. You can make multiple trades within a short two-hour window. Some traders open and close positions in a matter of seconds. The same goes for the last hour and a half prior to market closing. This is a perfect time to liquidate any open positions. However, you need to be careful as the market selloff right before the end of the day may cause you to take a cut on your profits.

Time Management

Time management is about being consistent. Investing time daily to develop your craft is ideal. If you only go over charts or look at your trading platform once or twice a week, you may be surprised to find that your results aren't what you expect them to be. As a result, being consistent in the amount of time you spend is key.

Most successful day traders spend about two to three hours a day on their trading platform in addition to any time they spend on research. If you have a full-service account, much of the research is done for you. So, all you have to do is go over your news feed to see where you want to place your trades. You can then set up the system to take care of everything for you.

Core Components

Every good strategy regardless of its structure must have the following three components. These components are always present. Therefore, you cannot ignore them. If you fail to acknowledge them, they'll come back to bite you. So, it's best to take care of them right away. Doing so will help you avoid a myriad of problems later on.

Liquidity

Liquidity refers to the ease you would have to buy and sell an asset. Some assets are highly liquid while others are not. This term refers to how easily you could sell something especially in times of turmoil. For example, a house is a great example of an illiquid asset. After all, you can't expect to sell a house in five minutes. It may take weeks, even months, before you get a good offer.

Highly liquid assets include desirable stocks (blue-chip companies like Apple, Facebook, or GM), commodities (gold, oil), or currencies. Depending on the nature of the asset, you may have offers already lined up. So, make sure to focus on liquid assets.

In contrast, illiquid assets may be highly profitable but hard to move during a market downturn. For instance, real estate, intellectual property, or industrial assets are all valuable but hard to find buyers. These assets are much better for a buy and hold strategy as opposed to a short-term one.

Volatility

Volatility refers to the amount of trading volume occurring at any point. For example, volatility picks up at the beginning of the trading day. This is a natural occurrence derived from the entry of all players into the game.

Volatility can also increase when there are unexpected events in the economy. These events can come in the form of government policy, natural disasters, or poor economic data. However, these events may also be positive. If they are positive events, volatility may pick up in terms of buying rather than selling.

When volatility is low, you may not have the chance to make significant gains. Therefore, an HFT approach is best. If volatility is high, you might find that undervalued companies may rise to the occasion. So, it's best to find undervalued companies before volatility picks up. Then, when volatility rises, you can sell amid the frenzy.

Volume

Volume refers to the number of times an individual has been traded during a specific time frame. Volume in an indication of how liquid a stock is. As such, the lower the volume, the less popular the stock is. Therefore, you might have trouble selling it in a short time window. In contrast, if a stock has a high trading volume, then you can confidently but it and sell it whenever you need to. This is the core indicator you need to look at when considering an individual stock for HFT.

Most Successful Day Trading Strategies

Let's take a look at the most successful day trading strategies. These strategies can help you make a great deal of money when executed correctly. In some cases, you can hit it out of the park. Please note that these strategies are not always suited for HFT. So, you may have to hold on to stocks for a few hours as opposed to a few minutes. Nevertheless, the profits can make up the difference.

1. **Breakout**

This strategy refers to stock breaking past a specific upper limit. A stock's upper limit is known as a "resistance level." This is a psychological barrier in which investors are unwilling to surpass. In other words, investors feel that this point makes the stock too expensive. However, there are times in which investors are waiting for an event before deciding to buy up the stock. For example, investors may be waiting for economic data from the government. If the data is positive, they jump in. If the data is bad, they will hold.

Entry point: To determine your entry point in this trade, take a look at the stock's price history. If you find that it was at a higher price point previously, you have a reference to where the price could land. The stock is poised to break out when you see its price hit the resistance level but not surpass it. After three successive hits on a resistance level, the stock may be ready to achieve a breakthrough. While the timing is unpredictable, indications are that it will happen very quickly. So, do keep this in mind.

Exit point: The exit point of your trade is any point above the resistance level. A good rule of thumb is to place your sell price at a reasonable level. For example, anything close to or at its previous high is a good idea. Unless there is reason to believe that the price will break past its previous highs, you are better off sticking to its previous high. Depending on your entry point, you could really make a killing.

2. **Reversal**

A reversal is when a stock's price is trending downward, levels off, and the rises. The opposite is also true. Therefore, reversals are highly useful as both entry and exit points. To execute this strategy, you need to be aware of the stock's price history. Based on this, you can determine if and when a reversal in trend will take place.

Let's consider a downward trend. This is also called a "bearish" trend. When there is a bearish trend, a stock's price will eventually fall to a specific point and then rebound. It can be quite difficult to predict the exact point in which it will happen. But with the use of technical analysis, you can spot the point in which trend is about to reverse.

To spot the reversal, you must look at the point in which the trendline stops falling and then flattens out. Then, you can see the point in which the trendline will begin to rise. Sometimes, the trendline will have a "V" shape. This means it falls, hits a point, and then bounces back up immediately. The point right before the price begins to rebound is your optimal entry point. Therefore, this is the lowest price you can buy before the stock begins to rise.

In the opposite scenario, you have a "bullish" trend. This type of trend means the price is rising to a point in which it will come back down. The point right before the price drops back down is your optimal sell point. As such, this is the point where you'll make the most profit.

When you use reversals, you can buy at the lowest possible point and then sell at the highest possible price. This is how you can maximize profits.

3. Momentum or piggybacking

In this strategy, you are "riding the wave." It is best executed when there is news that alters investors' perceptions. For example, a company announces better-than-expected earnings. So, as soon as you hear the news, you buy it. As the wave rises, you sell. This will help you make some quick profits. However, you need to be careful not to wait too long. In this strategy, investors want to rise to the highest part of the wave. The problem is that waiting too long may set you up for a precipitous crash. In the best of cases, you'd see your profits reduced. In the worst of cases, you might end up losing money on the deal. Therefore, piggybacking is about entering quickly, making a profit, and then pulling out. It is a very short-term strategy. Thus, you must be ready to act quickly. Riding on momentum is relatively predictable especially during earnings season. It's a perfect way to make some quick funds during moments of increased volatility and volume.

The same can also be done when a stock pulls back. Often, stocks drop in price right before rising. This is commonly referred to as "buying on the dip." This strategy allows for short-term gains especially when there is a high degree of volatility. So, keep your eyes open for these movements. They can prove to be quite profitable in the short term.

Chapter 7: Fundamentals of Swing Trading

Swing trading is another approach investors use to maximize profits. This approach calls for more patience as investors are looking toward a longer time frame. As such, swing trading goes beyond the one-day time frame of day trading. With swing trading, investors hold open positions for periods ranging from a few days to several weeks.

The main purpose of swing trading is to capitalize on market "swings." Since we're looking at a longer time frame, we're anticipating much larger swings in price action. Instead of focusing on price action that shifts in pennies, we're anticipating much larger swings. Depending on the size of a position, this could represent hundreds, if not thousands of dollars.

Difference Between Day and Swing Trading

On the whole, day and swing trading work in the same way. The same type of trading platform is used. Also, the same techniques and analytical tools are used. The main difference lies in the time frame in which trades are placed. Day trading calls for opening and closing positions within the same trading session. In swing trading, you need to be prepared to keep your positions open for a much longer time frame. However, this is how you maximize profit.

Another important difference lies in the use of risk/reward ratios. In essence, a risk/reward ratio is based upon a potential loss versus a potential gain. Naturally, if the gain outweighs the loss, then the deal is worth entering. For instance, a good rule of thumb is a 3:1 risk to reward ratio. In other words, you stand to make $3 while risking a loss of $1. In the case of day trading, risk to reward ratios doesn't make much sense as the trade is so short-term.

It's also worth mentioning that swing trading requires patience. You need to be willing to sit and wait for market swings to occur. They are highly unpredictable. Therefore, you need to ready to wait until you reach your desired price points. Otherwise, you may exit the trade before achieving your desired price point.

Use Technical Analysis and Fundamental Analysis

Technical analysis is the use of quantitative tools to analyze price action information. Here, we're talking about price, volatility, and volume. These indicators provide objective data you can use to base your decisions. As a result, you're not basing your investment choices on hunches.

Fundamental analysis is the study of non-quantitative factors that influence price action. These are mainly economic, political, and most importantly, psychological factors. Fundamental analysis is essential when looking at a long-term picture. For example, political decisions by the government influence investors' mindset. Consequently, when investors become uneasy about potential shifts in the market, they may choose to sit on the sidelines. By the same token, if the outlook is positive, you may find investors jumping into the fray. Therefore, a close study of fundamental analysis is essential in any successful swing trading strategy.

To be successful at swing trading, you need to become familiar with both technical analysis and fundamental analysis. Therefore, swing trading requires a greater

31

commitment in terms of time and effort. You need to pay close attention to market conditions. This will enable you to foresee opportunities. When you get really good at spotting future swings, you can make considerable profits.

Advantages of Swing Trading

Let's take a look at the advantages that come with swing trading.

1. **Swing trading requires less time than day trading**

Even though you need a greater commitment of time and effort in conducting research, the overall amount of time required to engage in swing trading is much less. The reason for this lies in the time it takes to set up trades. In day trading, you need to be at your computer every day, setting up trades, and monitoring your positions.

In the case of swing trading, you set up trades with a longer time frame. Therefore, you won't be placing nearly as many trades. If you plan on doing a combination of day and swing trading, you would still be making fewer trades. Thus, you could conceivably set up trades, and go for days without touching any of your positions. In the meantime, you would be free to continue your research.

2. **Profit maximization**

You stand to make much more profits as you ride large waves as opposed to short-term times. These large waves are the result of capturing significant swings in the market. By spotting these potential swings early on, you can set yourself up for massive gains.

3. Decisions are based on technical analysis

In swing trading, technical analysis will tell you what you can expect. While there is certainly a place for hunches, you must base all of your decisions on technical analysis. As such, you'll be able to spot reversals in trend, changes in trading volume, or the emergence of resistance and support levels. Therefore, you need to pay close attention to the fundamentals of technical analysis.

Disadvantages of Swing Trading

Now, let's take a look at the disadvantages that come with swing trading.

1. You are vulnerable to risk

Since you have open positions for longer time frames, you are open to greater risk, particularly with overnight markets. Since developments can occur at any time, you might wake up one morning to a drastically different landscape. Thus, the use of stop-loss triggers is vital to ensuring you don't get wiped out in a single trade.

2. Sudden market reversals

Since markets are relatively unpredictable, any sudden changes can expose you to significant risk. As such, you need to ensure that you are aware of the potential risks. This situation implies that you must use stop-loss or take-profit triggers to ensure that you capture your desired price points.

3. Short-term trends outweigh long-term ones

Even though swing trading has a longer time frame than day trading, it's still a short-term approach. As such, swing traders are more focused on short-term profits rather than long-term ones. This is a necessary approach as swing traders are looking to make as much money as possible in the least amount of time. Since there is no telling what can happen, it's best to cash out as soon as your desired price points are hit.

Are you enjoying this book? If so, i'd be really happy if you could leave a short review on Amazon, it means a lot to me! Thank you!

Chapter 8: How to Succeed at Swing Trading

To be successful at swing trading, you need to become highly familiar with technical analysis. This will be the cornerstone of your strategy. Thus, you must do your homework by consistently checking in on price charts. Based on your observation and analysis, you'll be able to determine what stocks are ripe for the plucking.

However, you don't need to have a crystal ball to figure everything on your own. Lots of investors rely on experts' advice and analysis. You hear these pundits on television or read their columns. They can provide you with insight and knowledge that you may not have been familiar with. As such, it's always good to listen. Nevertheless, always take what they say with a grain of salt.

Mainly, it's important for you to take everything you hear and read and verify the information with your analysis. As a result, you can contrast the opinions you get from the media. Additionally, analytics services like Bloomberg or Market Watch provide an expert recommendation. These analyses are generally available to subscribers only. So, you might want to consider purchasing a subscription. While it is not necessary for you to purchase one, you might want to consider it anyway. The best course of action would be a free trial. That way, you can see if the information is worth the money you would be paying for it.

Swing Trading Strategies

Swing trading strategies require you to dig deeper into the history and trend of price action. This is important as historical data will help you glean into the patterns the stock is trading. When you learn to spot these patterns, you can anticipate what will happen with reasonable accuracy. Anyone who masters technical analysis can predict what will happen. The only thing you need to be aware of is that predict time is nearly impossible. Of course, ballpark estimations are certainly reasonable. However, it's virtually impossible to determine the date and time market shifts will take place. Therefore, you must think twice before believing anyone who claims they can "time" the market.

To make the most of the strategies we will describe herein, please take the time to go over historical data. Most financial news services will provide you with historical data on stock prices. Many will go back at least 10 years. Although, you would only need two or three years' worth of data at most. Going back this far will allow you to determine patterns and trends in stock prices. From there, you will find patterns emerging.

To establish these patterns, you must become familiar with an indicator known as the "moving average."

Moving Average

The moving average is an indicator that is calculated based on historical data. In short, a moving average is the average between the buy and sell price in a given time frame. Depending on the chart, this could be presented on an hourly or daily basis. Some highly specialized real-time charts may present moving average information on a minute-by-minute basis. However, this is not as common as reading hourly data.

Investors and traders use the moving average as a means of determining the overall trend in the price of a stock. Thus, there are three possible types of trends: bearish, bullish, and flat.

A bullish trend means that the price of the stock is rising. While you will find that that chart reflects ups and downs in the overall price action of a stock, the trendline indicates that the price of the stock is rising. Therefore, you can consider this is a bullish trend. Now, it might be impossible to determine how high the price will go. To get an idea, look at previous highs. That should give you an indication of how high the price can go. Unless the stock is experiencing a breakout, you can expect it to fall somewhere around its previous high.

A bearish trend is the opposite of a bullish one. In a bearish trend, the moving average indicates that the price is falling. Hence, you can use this information to either plan an entry point, or stay away from the stock until its price action settles down. Bearish trends usually emerge when the overall trend in the market is down. Nevertheless, individual stocks may fall even though the overall trend in the market is bullish.

A flat or sideways trend means there is no clearly defined trend. As such, it is neither bearish nor bullish. This situation generally indicates that investors are sitting on their hands. In other words, investors are looking to avoid entering the market or selling their positions. This reaction, or lack thereof, is the result of an uncertain situation. When investors don't know what to expect, they may delay making trades as long as possible. To capitalize on a sideways trend, you need to look at the trend leading up to the sideways action. For example, if the trend was bullish, but then it leveled off, you might expect a sharp downturn. In contrast, if the trend was bearish and the leveled off, you might expect a reversal into a bullish one. Unless you have a reasonable belief that the previous trend will continue, the likeliest scenario is that prices will eventually reverse.

10-Day and 20-Day Simple Moving Average

A great tactic swing traders use is called the "simple moving average." This tactic is used as a means of calculating the average daily price of a stock by "smoothing" it out. The term "smoothing" is used in statistics to refer to the process of eliminating fluctuations from a data set. When fluctuations are eliminated, it is possible to see where the overall trend of the data set lies.

To do this, two separate measures are used the 10-day and the 20-day simple moving average. The reason for using these measures lies in using historical data to predict future short-term shifts. Thus, if you want to look at long-term shifts, then you need to look at long-term data such as the 50-day and 200-day moving average.

To produce the simple moving average indicator, all you need to do is add up the average price of the last ten days. After adding them up, divide them by 10. This will give you the average price of the last 10 days. Now, take two separate sets, that is 20 days, and add them together. If you find a divergence between the two indicators, then you have a signal.

A buy signal is sent when the 10-day simple moving average is greater than the 20-day one. This indicates that the price is rising. In contrast, if the 10-day simple moving average is lower than the 20-day one, you must sell. This indicates that the price is heading downward.

You can use this tactic as a means of determining your entry and exits points. Let's assume you don't hold any position. You spot the buy signal, so you set your entry point. Then, you hold until you see the next 10-day moving average cross the 20-day. Once you get the sign to sell, you immediately liquidate your position.

Now, does this mean you have to wait another 10 days before you sell?

No, you don't have to. What you do is you calculate the 10-day moving average every day. All you do is eliminate the 10th day and add the last day. This is why it's called a "moving" average. By doing this, you can spot the exact point in which the price action flashes either a "sell" or "buy" signal.

Moving Average Convergence Divergence Crossover

The moving average convergence divergence (MACD) is commonly used in swing trading to help investors pinpoint when to buy or sell. Unlike the simple moving average, the MACD flashes signals based on two lines, the moving average line (trendline) and the signal line. Most charts represent these are red and blue. Although, you might find any number of color combinations.

The MACD is automatically generated by most stock tracking charts. Also, they are generally available for free. So, you don't need to get an expensive subscription package to have access to these indicators. To take advantage of these indicators, you need to pay attention to the points in which the lines cross one another. This is called a "crossover." Depending on the trend, this will indicate a sell or buy signal.

For instance, when the MACD line crosses over (higher) the signal line, then this indicates the trend is bullish. Therefore, it is a signal to buy. You can also determine this visually as the lines themselves are moving upward. When the MACD line crosses belove (lower) the signal line, then this is a sell line as you can anticipate a bearish trend. Of course, this signal can also be an indication of a "buy" signal if you don't hold an open position. All you have to do is keep an eye on the lines right before the intersect again. This is the lowest price you could buy.

It is important to keep in mind that if you sell after the MACD cross over occurs at the top of the trendline, then you would have missed out on the highest possible returns.

Hence, you need to sell right before the lines intersect. This will provide you with the highest possible returns.

Breakout Strategy

The breakout strategy is when you anticipate the price of a stock to blow past its previous highs. To make this strategy work, you need to use the 10-day average to keep a close eye on the stock's overall trend.

Here's how it works.

1. First, identify the trend in the stock of your choice. The trend must be a bullish one. A stock with a bearish trend will not work in this case. If anything, a stock with a bearish trend may break through its floor.

2. Second, look for a double top or triple top pattern. This pattern consists of two or three successive hits upon the stock's upper limit. You must spot at least two hits. If you spot three consecutive hits, then the breakout is imminent.

3. Third, set up your trade. Generally speaking, there is no telling how high the breakout will go. So, it's best to play it safe. You may find that the stock pulls back before continuing to rise. Consequently, you must strive to sell before the pullback. You can always sell, then buy on the pullback, and sell on the new rise.

4. Lastly, cash out as soon as you see your price point hit. It doesn't matter if the stock continues to rise. It's best to liquate your position before the pullback. Otherwise, your profits may be reduced completely.

With the breakout strategy, you must be aware of the resistance level in the stock. In general, the breakout is imminent when the trading volume dries up. This means that very few trades are being placed compared to the previous volume. The reason for this is generally due to investors expecting a specific action. For example, this action may be government data or some other event.

The most important thing to watch for is greed. Please avoid overriding your take-profit points. There is no telling when the stock's price might pull back. When this happens, the stock may regress before taking off again. Thus, you need to sell before the pullback and then re-enter your position when the stock pulls back. That way, you can capture the new rise.

On the whole, the breakout strategy is the most successful strategy that investors use to make substantial profits. If you can capture a stock at its lowest point, and then ride the wave all the way past the breakout, you are in great shape to make substantial gains. This is the reason why swing trading is all about making patience and timing. Additionally, you must become familiar with technical analysis. Otherwise, it will be very difficult for you to capture the positive swings in the market.

Chapter 9: Fundamentals of Position Trading

Position trading is the longest-term approach in stock trading. This is where investors are willing to lay their money down for a longer time frame in hopes of capturing significant shifts in the market or individual stocks. As a result, position traders don't really care too much about the ups and downs of day-to-day trading. They are more concerned about the big picture. Consequently, position traders are far likelier to look at trades happening in terms of weeks and months rather than days.

It's worth noting that position traders are not passive investors. Passive investors are the ones who employ the "buy and hold" strategy. As such, passive investors simply put their money into an investment and wait for the return at some point. In contrast, position investors are focused on the trend. This approach implies that the trend will lead to the investor's ultimate goal. Therefore, technical analysis and fundamental analysis play a huge role in determining how a trade will be set up.

Understanding Long-Term Trend

In stock trading, any time frame that surpasses a month is considered long-term. In swing trading, it is not surprising to find investors holding their positions for over a month. However, they rarely hold open positions for any period longer than 30 days. Anything after 30 days would fall into the realm of position trading.

The long-term trend is all about identifying where the price of an individual stock may go. This often implies that you need to ride out short-term fluctuations and pullbacks. As a result, you may actually lose value before reaching your ultimate target. This is the reason why position trading is not for investors seeking short-term profits. Position trading is for those who are concerned with truly maximizing their profits.

Typically, position traders aren't overly active. They may place anywhere between 10 to 20 trades per year. However, those trades make should make enough money to offset the time it takes for them to pay off. In the end, position trading provides investors with a lucrative opportunity to cash in on the big picture market shifts.

Advantages of Position Trading

Here are the most significant advantages of position trading

1. Position trading doesn't demand much time

Position trading requires upfront planning. However, once the trade is set up, all the investor needs to do is monitor the situation. Once the conditions unfold, the investor can then execute the transaction. Therefore, this trading approach does not require a great deal of time to pursue.

2. Profit maximization

Long-term trends generally yield the highest returns. In short-term trading, profit margins can be limited to a few pennies on the dollar. In long-term trading, profits can be several dollars per share. So, when you multiply them over a large number of shares, profits truly add up.

3. Risk management

Position trading offers investors the opportunity to manage risk more carefully. In particular, short-term fluctuations are meaningless. Therefore, slight pullbacks are not of concern.

As a matter of fact, short-term fluctuations are just a part of the deal. This approach offers greater flexibility. This enables investors to cash out in case they need to leave their position at any time.

Disadvantages of Position Trading

Position trading also has its disadvantages. So, let's take a look at them.

1. Money is tied up for a long time

The duration of trades is the biggest disadvantage of position trading. Some investors are not interested in keeping their money tied up for so long. As such, they would much rather engage in shorter-term deals. This enables them to move their money around, thereby generating smaller, but more consistent profits.

2. There are no guarantees

While position trading offers the possibility of significant returns, there is no guarantee they will materialize. This situation leads investors to think twice about investing their money for any period beyond three or four weeks. Also, it is worth noting that conditions can change overnight. As a result, investors are always exposed to risk.

3. Opportunity cost

The term "opportunity cost" refers to the choice you need to make between one thing or another. In this case, you choose to invest in a stock over another. While this is a common decision investors frequently make, investing over a longer time frame magnifies this situation. For instance, investing in a stock for three months means you can't use those funds to trade other stocks throughout that time frame. Thus, your options suddenly become limited. This is the reason why the profits from position trading need to outweigh short-term profits made through day and swing trading.

Combined Strategy

If you consider using position trading as part of a combined strategy, you can truly make your portfolio go into high gear. Hence, you can use position trading as part of a diversified portfolio. For example, you can be a dedicated day trader looking for consistent, short-term gains. Then, you can use swing trading to capitalize on trend reversals and breakouts. Lastly, you can use position trading to capture larger market shifts, especially when you can't quite pinpoint when these shifts will happen.

The main advantage of having a diversified portfolio lies in ensuring that you capture the various time frames the market has to offer. When you have your portfolio spread out over various strategies, you will find that you can make money on a consistent basis.

As for risk, diversification allows you to manage it more effectively. If you place all of your investment capital in a position trading approach, it will be hard for you to make consistent returns. If you neglect long-term market movements, you may miss out on short-term opportunities. Hence, making use of all timeframes helps you capture the bulk of the market's price action.

Lastly, position trading is a great way to invest money, particularly when you are more focused on the big picture. This big-picture approach gives you the opportunity to correct your strategy on the fly. You can enter and exit trades within a reasonable time frame. With short-term investing, you have to roll with the punches. As a result, position trading gives you a higher degree of flexibility as part of your overall strategy.

Chapter 10: How to Succeed at Position Trading

Being successful in position trading is all about anticipating market movements. Since it's impossible to determine the exact moment in which movements will happen, you need to be ready to capitalize at any time. This is the reason why the position remains open for so long. You don't know when prices will go up or down. Nevertheless, you set up your trades so that you're ready for them.

Since you are looking for trends, the main thing is to be ready for the signals that may indicate a reversal. If you are holding a position, you need to be ready for a possible reversal. In this possible reversal, you will get a signal indicating a sale. If you are looking to enter a trade, then a reversal in a bearing trend will indicate your entry point. This is the core strategy around position trading. The issue here is figuring out at what point you need to enter and exit trades.

Like swing trading, position trading uses the moving average as its main technical analysis tool. The difference is that instead of looking at the 10-day or 20-day moving average, we're going to be looking at the 50-day and 200-day moving average.

50-Day and 200-Day Moving Average

These indicators are exactly like the other indicators we discussed earlier. The difference is the time frame they analyze. Analyzing a longer time frame enables you to see the broader trend in a stock. This will help you determine if the price action you have seen is part of the stock's overall trend or not.

For instance, a stock falls sharply in a span of three trading days. On the surface, this movement indicates the stock is in a bearish trend. However, when you look at the 50-day moving average, you can see the stock is actually up. Therefore, this sharp decline is a pullback.

Now, if you are looking to confirm your observations, then you must look at the 200-day moving average. In this indicator, you can confirm the observations from the 50-day moving average. As such, you can confirm the trend or determine it to be the opposite.

Another common situation is steep increases. A stock may show significant increases over a few trading sessions. Yet, the stock is actually down over the 200-day period. Therefore, you can conclude that it's in a bearish trend. The increase in price may simply be the result of market momentum but not a reflection on this stock's true valuation.

These are the observations that you can make when looking at longer time frames. A day trader would not be concerned with these longer-term trends. A day trader would only be interested in seeing the price action over the shorter time frame. As a result, they could capitalize on the fluctuation in the price over one or two trading sessions. Moreover, a swing trader would bank on the movements occurring over three or four trading sessions without really paying much attention to what occurred prior to that.

In position trading, it is important to keep an eye on the big picture. As long as you keep your eyes on the larger scope of the market, you'll be able to spot the potential to make money. So, you should not neglect the way the markets move in addition to individual stocks. This will provide you with the best chance to make serious returns.

Determining Entry and Exit Points

You can use the 50-day and 200-day moving averages in an MACD crossover pattern. In this case, you execute your entry and exit points based on the trendline and the MACD line. When these lines cross over, you can establish your entry and exit points.

Let's consider a bullish trend. In this situation, you have an open position. As such, you are anticipating a climb in the stock's price. You must look at the overall trend, that 200-day moving average, to determine if there is a bullish or bearish trend. Since the 200-day moving average signals a bullish trend, you must wait for the moment in which both lines intersect. At the point in which the 50-day moving average crosses the 200-day moving average, then you have an exit point. This is the point at which you must sell.

At this point, two things can happen. The first thing is a possible trend reversal. The second is a flattening of the trendline. In either case, you stand to see your profit reduced. Thus, you must liquidate your position as close to the intersection point as possible.

In the case of a bearish trend, the point in which the 50-day intersects the 200-day moving average is your optimal entry point. This is the lowest point the stock will hit before bouncing up. As a result, you stand to make the largest profit. If you get into the trade too soon, the price of your stock will fall even further before it rebounds. This situation may cause you to become impatient. Plus, your profit would not be optimal as you could have bought the stock at a lower point. Consequently, you must try your best to get in at the point closest to the intersection of both moving averages.

Pullback and Retracement Strategy

Pullbacks are temporary dips that stocks experience during a bullish trend. Pullbacks can happen for any number of reasons. As such, it's important to look at the overall picture.

When you can clearly spot the overall bullish trends, pullbacks provide great opportunities to pick up shares at a cheaper. While the ideal approach is to get in at the lowest point of the trend, you can still capitalize on pullbacks to augment your position.

Position traders use pullbacks all the time to make shorter-term trades, much like swing trading, to generate some additional income while they wait for the big trade to come through. So, these dips in price can provide you with the opportunity to make some immediate profits particularly when you are looking to ride the overall trend.

A retracement is a type of pullback. It is a temporary dip in the price. The difference is that retracements follow a specific pattern. This pattern allows you to determine where the price will fall. Thus, you can plan the points at which you can place additional trades.

The most popular type of retracement strategy is known at the "Fibonacci" retracement. A Fibonacci retracement is based on the classic Fibonacci sequence. When this sequence is applied to a stock chart, you can determine entry and exit points for your trades. Please bear in mind that the overall trend is not expected to change. As such, you are still expecting to ride the wave all the way to the top. Nevertheless, a Fibonacci retracement provides you with the opportunity to plot your movements more accurately.

Here's how it works.

The Fibonacci retracement strategy is based on the Fibonacci sequence of 1, 2, 3, 5, 8, 13, 21, 34, 55, etc. This sequence is present throughout various elements of nature. When applied to stock trading, it enables you to plot specific price points in a chart. Consequently, you can reasonably assume where a price point may be useful to you.

It may seem incredible that stock market fluctuations act according to a similar pattern as the Fibonacci sequence.

This is the reason why the Fibonacci retracement strategy is quite useful. Of course, it's not infallible, but produces a lot of positive results most of the time.

The Fibonacci retracement strategy is calculated by placing six lines on a price chart. To do this, you need to take a price chart over any time frame. For the purpose of position trading, you can use a 50-day or 200-day chart. However, you could use a daily chart with hourly price points if you wanted to.

The first two lines correspond to the 100% and 0% levels. The 100% level corresponds to the highest price point in the chart while the 0% corresponds to the lowest. Based on this, you will now plot the 23.6%, 38.2%, 50%, and 61.8% levels. The 50% level corresponds to the exact middle of the chart. Hence, you would add the highest and lowest prices, and then divide them by two. This would give you the exact middle. The 23.6% and 38.2% would represent potential entry points. The 61.8% would be a good exit point. Some investors also like to plot the 75% level as a reference point.

To calculate your entry points, look at how many times the price points intersected at the 23.6% and 38.2% levels. If you find that the price points intersect several times, then you have potential entry points you can rely on. Then, take a look at the 61.8% level as this would be your likeliest exit point.

If you find that none of the points plotted in the Fibonacci retracement strategy intersects with the actual price points in the chart, then you are better off waiting for the overall trend to hit the mark you are expecting. Generally speaking, this is due to a high degree of volatility. Still, Fibonacci retracements are rarely off the mark. So, they can provide you with great reference points.

Resistance Levels and Breakouts

Whenever you experience a breakout, a new resistance level is set. This means that the price of a stock breaks out of its current resistance level and then settles at a higher price point. Therefore, the floor on the stock elevates while a new, much higher resistance level, is set.

This strategy is great because it allows you to determine where new price points can guide your trades. Consider this situation.

A stock currently trading at $11 a share has a support level of $9 and a resistance level of $12. As such, you expect this price to break past the $12 barrier due to technical and fundamental factors. Sure enough, the price bolts past $12 and hits a new high of $15. At this point, you expect the new resistance level to settle somewhere around the $14 to $15 range. After multiple spikes and pullbacks, there are three consecutive hits on the $14.50 mark. Consequently, you determine this to be the new resistance level.

Now, there is also a new support level. This means that the floor of the stock has now been raised from $9 to $11. This is important to note as you now expect the stock's price to hit $11 and then bounce back up. Here, you can use the "triple bottoms" indicator. This is exactly the same as the triple tops. You have three consecutive hits on the floor. This will determine the support level.

At this point, you can now confidently ride a rangebound trading strategy. Since you now have a reasonable belief regarding the range in which the stock will trade, you can place your next trades based on the new floor and ceiling.

This type of approach can be measured by using the 50-day and 200-day moving average. As such, you have enough data to determine how the trade will play out. Considering the length of the trade, you stand to make much more profit as compared to a day trading or swing trading approach.

Please keep in mind that all position trading strategies look to maximize profits based on historical data. If you base your trades on hunches, you may find that the price points you have anticipated may never materialize. Unless you have some reason to believe a stock that has never hit triple digits will do so at some point, then you are better off making your trades based on historical data. While the stock may reach the price point you expect, it may take years to get there. This is the reason why it is better to base your assumptions on real data. Otherwise, you may find yourself with an open position for far too long.

Only blue-chip stocks would be worth holding on to for any period greater than six months. Any other stock may become vulnerable to significant fluctuations. Naturally, this would pose unnecessary risk.

Chapter 11: Value Investing

Professional investors use value investing as a way to make under-the-radar moves. In value investing, investors search for value where others may not see it. Consequently, value investing is all about finding hidden gems.

This investment approach is quite popular among some of the most famous investors in the world. Warren Buffet, Benjamin Graham (Buffet's mentor), Charlie Munger, and David Dodd, among others, have built their investment strategy around value investing.

In essence, value investing consists of finding companies whose market value is below their intrinsic or book value. As such, these are companies that may have fallen on hard times but are poised to rebound at some point. Therefore, you must make an effort to go through financials and price history to determine a company's potential.

Determining Intrinsic Value

A company's intrinsic value is the value of its share capital based on its accounting. This means that a company is really worth what its accounting indicates. What you pay for in the open market is what investors believe it is worth. As such, there is always a difference between both numbers.

To determine a company's intrinsic value, all you need to do is take a company's total share capital and divide it by the number of outstanding shares. For instance, a company's total share value is $1,000,000. There are 100,000 outstanding shares. Therefore, 1,000,000 / 100,000 = 10. This means that each share is worth $10,

A company's intrinsic value changes very little over time. As a matter of fact, it's hard for companies to modify their intrinsic value as there are laws and accounting practices in place that limit this. Therefore, companies must be careful to follow proper accounting principles to ensure they are compliant with laws.

Determining Market Value

At the outset of this book, we explained how a company's market valuation depends on what investors believe the share price is worth. This is the reason why it changes so much in such a short time frame. Therefore, investors determine market value as a result of technical analysis. Of course, there are psychological factors involved. These factors determine whether a stock's valuation rises or falls.

Generally speaking, successful companies have a higher market valuation than intrinsic valuation. This implies that investors are prepared to pay more than the company is truly worth. The reasoning here is based on the company's potential for growth and profit.

When investors feel that a company is not performing up to expectations, its market valuation drops. In such cases, it's valuation may fall below its intrinsic value. In such cases, it could spell the end for the company. In many cases, companies don't rebound. Moreover, they may enter into bankruptcy proceedings. In some cases, companies emerge from restructuring. In others, the company is liquidated.

Spotting Potential Value

Spotting viable candidates for value investing takes time and research. Mainly, you need to pour over the company's financials. When you look at financials, you can get a glimpse into a company's overall health. If the company is generally profitable, but it is going through a tough time, then you can assume the company has a good chance of rebounding. By the same token, if you see bad financials, then the company may be headed for the glue factory.

Also, you must take a look at its price history. To get a good idea of where a company's valuation lies, look at its 200-day moving average. This will provide you with a very clear depiction of the company's true valuation. If you find that it has been in a bearish trend over the 200-day period, then you might be better off looking for another company. However, if you spot a clear moment where the stock took a downward turn, then you might have something.

Setting Up Your Trade

Please note that with value investing, there is no telling how long it will take a company to rebound. While it might take a few weeks, it might take a few months. It all depends on how quickly the company can rebound.

That being said, your entry point should be at the point where you see an MACD cross over. At this point, you will find the trendline crossing over the MACD line. When this happens, you might be on the verge of a trend reversal. Here, you must be ready to jump in and buy.

Next, it's time to determine your exit point. Technically, you could exit at any point above your entry point to make a profit. However, you are looking to maximize your profit. So, a good yardstick for your exit point would be to use the Fibonacci sequence. Look for the 61.8% level. This would be a very good exit point. Realistically, the 100% level may be unattainable, at least in the short term. As such, the 61.8% level would make perfect sense as it's slightly above the halfway mark of the stock's previous high. More conservative investors opt for the 50% level as an exit point.

Now, you can also use Fibonacci retracements to make multiple trades along the way. If the stock successfully rebounds, you can expect multiple pullbacks. Thus, using Fibonacci retracements can help you spot shorter-term trades.

On the whole, it is recommended that you make more conservative assessments. This is not the time to gamble. While it isn't easy to spot companies that might make a rebound, they can be quite profitable deals when you do spot them.

There is one caveat though. Please stay away from the so-called "penny stocks." Penny stocks are companies whose market valuation is less than $5. These are companies that are in liquidation. In the best of cases, they are zombie companies. This term means that they are still moving but not really going anywhere. As such, penny stocks are not worth your time as they will make very little profit if any. You could potentially make very short-term profits with penny stocks. However, it's best to look for companies which a much better chance of rebounding.

Conclusion

Thank you very much for making it all the way to the end of the book. If you're here, then it means you are serious about putting your money to work for you. By investing in the stock market, you are taking a huge step toward achieving your financial goals. As such, you are serious about making money without having to work any harder than you should.

So, what's the next step?

Please go over any sections of this book that you feel you need to review. Please keep in mind that reviewing specific parts of this book will help you improve your knowledge and experience. As you gain more and more experience, you'll be able to make the most of the information you have learned in this book.

It is also important to consider the options you have available to you. Often, it is not easy to make decisions given the vast array of options out there. This is the reason why it's important to ensure that you have all the information you need before making investment decisions. Moreover, please make sure that is careful with the so-called "gurus" and "experts." Thus, it is vital that you always verify the claims these individuals make. With this book, you can safely determine if the claims you hear are true or not.

The time has come for you to get started on the most exciting journey of your life. Stock market investing is the best way you can achieve your financial hopes and dreams. So, do take the time to carefully make your investment plan. As you set up your goals and aims, you will find that being realistic is the best place to start. As you gain more experience, you can set more ambitious goals. In the end, the sky is the limit when it comes to investing in the stock market.

Thank you once again for your time and dedication in reading this book. If you have found the information herein useful and informative, please tell your friends, colleagues, and family about it. They too will find this book to be useful. They will appreciate your sharing this information.

One last thing...

Stock market investing requires investors to do their homework. Please take the time to become familiar with technical analysis and fundamental analysis. The information you get from doing careful research will help you make the best possible investment decision. The good thing is that most of this research is done for you. Therefore, getting access to this information (usually through a subscription service) will help you make the most of the investment decisions you make. Often, spending a few extra dollars a month will make the difference between winning and losing trades.

Now that you're all set to go, please don't forget to have fun. In the end, if you enjoy investing, you will fare much better. By enjoying the time you spend investing, you will make much more money than you could have ever imagined!

Forex for beginners

The Ultimate Guide to Profitable Currency Trading

Gualtiero Favole

Introduction

Congratulations on purchasing *Forex for Beginners,* and thank you for doing so.

Did you know that the Forex market witnesses a $4 trillion trading volume every day? There are so many people who are investing in the Forex market, so why shouldn't you? You simply need a good internet connection and some basic knowledge to start, and in this book, you will be introduced to the concepts of Forex trading that will help you get started and make money. You don't even have to leave your day job if you want to invest in Forex. You can simply do it in your spare time. Start with a minimal sum, and you should practice with a demo account.

Once you read this book, you will have a comprehensive idea of how everything works here. You will get introduced to the main players and also figure out why the Forex market is so fascinating to everyone around the world. You will also know more about trading plans and strategies and how to have one for yourself. The Forex market has been there in existence for years, but now, it has become so popular mainly because of the presence of electronic trading, which has made the Forex market available to all. By the time you reach the end of this book, you will be ready and geared up to make your first trade.

There are plenty of books on this subject on the market, thanks again for choosing this one! Every effort was made to ensure it is full of as much useful information as possible, please enjoy!

Chapter 1: Introduction to the Forex Market

Before we go into the details of Forex trading, you need to have a basic knowledge about the Forex market, and that is exactly what we are going to do in this chapter. Forex or foreign exchange is being traded 24 hours every day for five days a week by institutions, banks, and individual traders all over the world. Another thing about Forex is that it does not have any centralized marketplace. So, at any point in time, whichever market is open, currencies are traded over-the-counter.

Thus, Forex is a global marketplace, and here, different national currencies are exchanged against each other. Finance, commerce, and trade have a worldwide grasp in today's world, and because of this, Forex is often considered to be the most liquid and largest asset markets around the globe.

What is the Forex Market?

The place where all the currency trading is done is termed as the forex market. People might not realize it that often but currencies are important to everyone irrespective of the country they live in. This is mainly because, in order to conduct business or foreign trade, the currency has to be exchanged. You, as a common civilian, might understand the importance of currency when you are traveling to a different country, for example, Thailand. If you are from the US, US dollars will not be accepted in Thailand. You have to exchange your US dollars into Thai baht, and only then can you purchase things there.

The major centers in terms of the forex market are

Zurich, Tokyo, New York, London, Hong Kong, Frankfurt, Sydney, and Paris. Now, as we said before, the forex market is open all day. When the trading day is coming to closure in the US, in Hong Kong and Tokyo, the forex market begins. Thus, there is no particular time in the day when you can say for certain that the forex market will remain highly active. It stays active any time of the day, and there is a constant fluctuation of the price quotes.

Types of Forex Markets

When broadly classified, there are two main markets in the foreign exchange category, and they are – spot market and forward market, and we are going to learn more about them in detail.

Spot Market

Among the different types of markets in Forex, here, you will find the quickest transactions. According to the present exchange rate, both sellers and buyers will get instant payment in this type of market. In fact, one-third of all the transactions happening in the forex market is part of the spot market, and for settling the transactions, usually 2-3 days are required by the traders. And because of this, the traders can stay open to the currency market's volatility. As a result of this, the price can either become less or rise between the trade and the agreement. When the deal of the currency is closed by the buyer and the seller within 2 days from the date of the deal, it is called a spot transaction. The spot exchange rate is referred to the rate at which the settlement of the transaction is done.

In the forex market, the volume of such spot transactions has increased a lot. These transactions usually happen through banking system transfers, cash-in of traveler's cheque, and trading of currency notes. But the most common one is the banking system transfer, which accounts for about 90% of the total transactions. These are specifically carried out by different banks.

Now, let us have a look at some of the main participants of these type of transactions –

- **Commercial Banks** – The first participant, which is also the main player in the spot market, is the commercial banks. This is because investment and commercial banks trade both for their customers and themselves. In fact, they aim at making a profit from exchange movements, and thus, the currencies put in by the bank are what make up the maximum portion of the transactions. If the volume of the transaction is huge, then the interbank transaction is also done. But when a small volume is involved, it might be done with the help of a broker.

- **Central Banks** – To reduce the fluctuations of the currency of a particular country, the central bank of that country will intervene in the foreign exchange market. Their aim is to ensure that the national economy's requirements and the exchange rate of their currency are compatible. In fact, the central banks might release some foreign currency into the market so that their own currency does not undergo any further depreciation. The appreciation of their currency is reduced by doing the reverse.

- **Brokers and Dealers** – Selling at high and buying at low are what dealers do. They are mainly involved in wholesale purchases, and in fact, they mostly perform interbank transactions. They might even deal with central banks and corporates from time to time. They have a very thin spread, and the costs involved in the transaction are quite low. As far as the overall value of deals in the forex market is concerned, 90% of them are wholesale transactions.

Forward Market

In the case of the forward market contract, a future date is decided by two entities or parties when the trade will be made at a stated quantity and price. When the deal is signed, there is no exchange of money, and so, no amount of security deposit is required. The trade is usually made after 90 days of the deal signing date.

Now, you might be wondering whether this type of contracting has any advantages or not. Well, there are some that you should know about – for starters, these types of contracts are mostly used in case of speculation and hedging. There are speculators in the market who study everything, perform thorough research, and then use that information to predict whether there will be an increase in the price. Then, if they do speculate that there will be an increase, they buy currencies in the forward market instead of buying in cash. After that, they would simply wait, and if their prediction is correct and the price increases, they would sell the currencies at a higher price, thus bringing home a handsome profit.

But along with these advantages, there are some disadvantages too. I have tried to explain them as concisely as possible –

- There are no centralized rules when it comes to trading in the forward market.
- Since only two parties are involved here, it is highly illiquid.

- The risk of default is always present, and so, there is counterparty risk.

In the first two problems that I have mentioned above, the presence of a lot of generality and flexibility is the main problem or point of concern for traders. It's like dealing with a real estate contract when only two persons are present. These two persons who are involved in the deal are the only ones who get to decide the terms of the contract based on what is convenient to them. If any of the two parties that are involved in the transaction declared bankruptcy, the other party would suffer, and this is known as counterparty risk, which is always present in the case of the forward market.

Another major point of concern while trading in the forward market is the time span and the fluctuations in that time span. The more the time span for which the contract is open, the greater will be the risk of huge movements in price. Thus, the counterpart risk present in the transactions keeps increasing.

Factors Affecting the Forex Market

The fluctuations and variations in the currency exchange rates that you see happen because of several factors that directly or indirectly affect the forex market. They lead to volatility, and if you want to enter the forex market, you need to know about these factors. Now that Forex has become a global marketplace, all the macroeconomic events happening across the world have a direct impact on the forex exchange rates. With modernization, you don't really have to remain concentrated on the popular currencies, but for someone who is starting out, the popular currencies are a good option. Overall, it is safe to say that any new information or current events can quickly affect the economic health of countries, and thus, the exchange rates. Below are some of the popular factors that you should keep in mind.

Political Landscape of a Country

The currency strength of any country is hugely affected by its economic performance and its political state. If political turmoil is less likely to happen in a country in the upcoming days, then foreign investors would be more interested in that country. This would mean that there would be an influx of foreign capital into that country, which, in turn, would lead the domestic currency to follow the path of appreciation. When the trade policy and financial condition of a country are in a sound place, they do not usually allow for any amount of uncertainty in their currency. But the exchange rates will witness frequent depreciation in the case of countries with political confusions.

When the government is willing to take the necessary steps to improve everything in a country, the economy will automatically flourish. Thus, investors look for countries that have a stable government because they know that such countries have a much higher chance of growth, and there would be very few roadblocks in their way. For example, when news of Brexit came out, the GBP suffered a dive in price compared to USD.

Inflation

I think this one shouldn't be of that much surprise because if there is something that lays a direct impact on the currency, then it is inflation. The currency value of a country will follow the path of appreciation if the inflation rate of that country is lower than that of the others. When the rate of inflation is low, there is a slow increase in the prices of different things. Similarly, if the rate of inflation in any country is high, then it's currency will follow a path of depreciation. Now, for an investor, a currency whose rate of inflation is lower would be attractive. For example, there was an aggressive devaluation of the Zimbabwe currency when the country went through a period of serious inflation, and so, in the forex market, the Zimbabwe currency does not hold an attractive place.

Interest Rates

The value of a currency and its exchange rates depends largely on the interest rates. Inflation, interest rates, and forex rates are three entities that are all interrelated. The currency of a country follows the path of appreciation when there is an increase in the interest rate because lenders get higher rates, which means there will be more influx of foreign capital.

Government Debt

The national debt or the public debt that the Central government owes is referred to as the Government debt. Foreign capital is not likely to enter a country that has a huge amount of government debt and this, in turn, leads to a rise in inflation. If a country has government debt, then the bonds will be sold in the open market by foreign investors. Thus, it will lead to a subsequent decrease in the exchange rate value.

Think of it in this way – if someone who already has a lot of debt comes to you asking for money, would you be willing to give it? No, right? The same thing is happening here. The government debt of a country over the past couple of years is studied by foreign investors before they decide to part with their money.

Country's Current Account

When a country makes a foreign investment, there is a balance of trade and earnings, both of which are reflected in the current account of the country. All the transactions of debt, imports, and exports are included here. Depreciation of the exchange rate happens when the country is not earning a sufficient amount through the sale of exports, but at the same time, it is spending huge amounts of money on importing certain products. The domestic currency exchange rate fluctuates depending on the balance of payments.

Terms of Trade

In simpler terms, the terms of trade are nothing but the ratio of export prices to that of the import prices. If the rate of increase in export prices is way more than that of import prices in a country, then there is an improvement in terms of trade. The direct result of this is that the revenue of the country improves. Thus, the value of the currency of that particular country also increases, and the currency is now high in demand. Thus, the exchange rate follows a path of appreciation.

If we see from the point of view of an investor, then they would be more interested in those countries which have lesser imports and more exports.

Speculation

Among all other factors, this is not really something that you can measure. The rate of a currency increases when there is speculation of its rate to increase in the coming days. Investors from all around the world will flock to the currency. But the catch here is that you have to identify this trend and also be out of it in time because if you stay inside it for too long and the trend ends, then you will be the one at a loss.

So, these were some of the factors that you should know about if you are planning to enter the forex market as they affect the exchange rates of different currencies.

Forex Trading vs. Stock Trading

Forex leverage is the first and foremost reason why so many people prefer forex trading over stock trading. In this section, we are going to discuss that, along with several other points.

Leverage

As far as stock trading is concerned, 2:1 leverage is used by the margin account traders. Although you have to keep in mind that people who perform day trading can also access leverage of as much as 4:1 because they open their positions and close them on the same day provided that their account balance is above $25,000. Apart from this, the 4:1 leverage can only be accessed once you have met a few other criteria as well. A margin account is not given to every investor, at least not right away, and in the case of stock trading, if you want to leverage, a margin account is mandatory.

But, let us come to forex trading – here, you do not need a margin account. If you want to use leverage in trading, you simply open a forex trading account. There are no requirements to be met. The leverage amount differs from one country to another. In USA, a 50:1 leverage is what your limit is, but there are countries where it can be leveraged to as much as 400:1.

Liquidity

As you might already know, in stock trading, you are basically buying the shares of different companies. The cost of these can vary a lot. It can be as low as tens of dollars to even hundreds of dollars. Demand and supply are what determines the price of these shares. But in the world of Forex, things are quite different. Yes, there are chances of fluctuation in the exchange rate of a country's currency, but even then, you will have a huge amount of currency at your disposal that you can use to trade. And this is why currency as an asset is highly liquid.

Paired Trades

The quotation for currencies in trading is always done in a pair. Thus, it simply means that you have to think about both countries and their economies – the country against whose currency you are trading and the country whose currency you have chosen.

The market also determines what you should be concerned about. Let us say that you have purchased Intel shares, then your main concern is not what is happening to other companies and their shares but whether or not there will be a rise in the value of the stock you hold. But if you see the scenario of the forex market, you have to be concerned about the economies of the countries whose currencies you are trading. Does one country have better political stability than the other? Does one of them have a better GDP or more job growth? These are the things that you will have to think about. Thus, there are two financial entities that you need to worry about when you are trading in the forex market and not just one.

Compared to stock trading, Forex is usually more sensitive to economic and political situations in other countries.

Trade Activity and its Effect on Price

The price sensitivity of the stock market with respect to trade activity varies greatly from that of the Forex market. The stock price might be impacted when 10,000 shares are purchased, especially when small companies are concerned. But for greater companies or giants like that of Apple, this would hardly scratch the surface.

On the contrary, the market price of the currency will not be affected even a bit even when there are a hundred million dollars of forex trades.

Market Accessibility

In comparison to stock markets, greater access is provided to the currency markets. Well, if we are to see the modern-day, then it is possible for you to trade stocks all throughout the day (24 hours) and for five days a week, but as far as the difficulty level is concerned, it won't be easy. But due to the presence of several forex exchanges spread across the world, you can do forex trading 24 hours a day and for six days a week with ease.

And lastly, the regulations will give you much more freedom in the forex market than it will give you in the stock market. But at the same time, it is these regulations in the stock market that give you a certain amount of protection that you cannot get in the forex market.

Chapter 2: Fundamental and Technical Analysis in Forex

When it comes to market analysis, there are two major types that you should be aware of – technical analysis and fundamental analysis. These two options are not mutually exclusive, but if you talk to any trader around you, everyone will fall into one of these two categories.

If we were to judge them from a neutral standpoint, I'd say that both have their own share of drawbacks as well as advantages. Here, in this chapter, we are going to learn more about both these types of analysis in detail.

Fundamental Analysis

If you want to make correct predictions as to whether the currency exchange rates are going to up or down, one of the methods of evaluation is termed fundamental analysis. The main idea behind fundamental analysis is that you have to study and do research about various macro-economic events and then figure out how they are affecting a particular currency. You also have to keep an eye on the social and political news and any monetary policy shifts. You have to make this analysis for both currencies in the currency pair.

Let us say that you are working with a regional currency, for example, Euro – in that case, you have to analyze the entire regional economy along with the member states so that your evaluation of the financial status of the region turns out to be accurate.

In short, whenever there are some changes in the geopolitical or economic nature of a country, currency pairs react at once. This reaction can turn out to be even more drastic when the change occurs in a way that was not initially expected. That is why a fundamental analysis of the market is of utmost importance so that you can understand the changes that are going to happen in the exchange rates in the near future and in which way the market is going to move.

Tools

Now, let us see what the different tools that are used in fundamental analysis in the forex market are. Firstly, there is historical data, then comes financial news from different types of media, and then there is the economic calendar.

The factors that can leave an impact on a national currency, be it any minor economic data or a major one, will be informed to the trader through the economic calendar. You will get to know the time and date of these releases. The financial news broadcasts that are done on various types of media will tell you whether there have been any major geopolitical event or any other economic change that you should be concerned about.

And then there are historical fundamental data through which you will get to know whether there was a similar economic situation in the country in the past and how the currency had reacted in that situation at that time.

Indicators

In this section, we are going to discuss some of the major indicators in the fundamental analysis that will help you understand whether a potential change in the exchange rate is coming or what the overall strength of the economy currently is. In fact, some of these indicators are so powerful and important that they might even be able to tell whether the economy is going to turn down or turn up any time soon.

So, let us see some of these important indicators in the forex market in more detail –

- **Trade Balance** – As I explained to you in the first chapter, the trade balance refers to the difference between the total exports and the total imports of a country. This particular indicator has a direct effect on the currency of the country and whether it is in demand or not. If the trade balance is more and there is a surplus, then it means that the country is doing good because the amount of imports is less than that of exports. On the other hand, if the trade balance is less and there is a deficit, then it means that the country is not performing well and the number of exports is less than that of the imports.

- **Employment Reports** – This refers to all kinds of data related to jobs – for example, the total number of claimants or applicants for a particular service, the unemployment rate, and also the levels of payrolls along with several other important things.

- **Current Accounts** – All the net cash transfers and balance of trade of a particular country are shown in the current accounts. If this amount shows a deficit, then it means that the country is neck-deep in debt. But if the amount is in surplus, then it shows that the total debts of the country are less than that of the total foreign assets.

- **GDP** – This stands for Gross Domestic Product, and the currency of a country depends largely on this value. The economy of a country is presumable in a good and stable state if there is an increase in GDP value, and this would also mean that the currency of the country would follow the path of appreciation. This is even stronger if there is a possibility of an increase in interest rates.

- **CPI** – This stands for Consumer Price Index, and this indicator is very important with respect to inflation. It acts on the consumer level and shows at what level the prices of different products are. The central banks of any country are highly focused on controlling the rate of inflation, and so, the monetary policies of the country can be influenced by CPI. The interest rates would increase when the rate of inflation increases, and at the same time, the interest rates would hit a low when the consumer prices are low.

- **PPI** – Before a finished product is made, the amount that the manufacturers are paying in order to get their raw materials is denoted by PPI or Producer Price Index. Now, you must be wondering how this affects the currency of a country. Well, it does, because higher consumer inflation in the future is indicated by a higher PPI value and vice-versa.

- **National Credit Quality** – There are major agencies around the world that give ratings to countries based on whether they have defaulted on their loans or they have the intention to repay them, and this will indicate the credit quality of that country. This would have a direct impact on the currency of the country.

- **Commodity Prices** – Next, we come to
  another important indicator that plays a vital role in
  identifying disinflationary and inflationary cycles in
  both consuming and producing nations. Let us take
  crude oil, for example. If the price of crude oil
  decreases, then the first impact would be on
  transport, and thus, the different goods' costs would
  also be influenced. The level of inflation would also be
  reduced. But the inflation would rise if the price of
  crude oil were to increase.

Advantages & Disadvantages

Now that you have a basic idea of what fundamental analysis is all about, we are going to check some of its advantages and disadvantages.

The advantages are –

- **Explanation of Price Movements** – Movements
  in price can happen very quickly, and as a beginner in
  the world of Forex, you might not always understand
  what is happening, and that is where fundamental
  analysis comes in. It will help you keep up with the
  economic reports and news, which are the major
  reasons behind price movements. The movements are
  even drastic when there is some unexpected economic
  change.

- **Finding Valuation** – There is a specific value for
  every asset or financial instrument. So, you as a
  trader will have to go through these values, and if you
  find that the current market price
  and the true value of an asset have discrepancies,
  then it is your job to find that out. The fundamental
  analysis gives you the scope of going through

industrial production, consumer sentiment, inflation, interest rates, and so on, all of which help you to find out asset values.

- **Understand Global Markets** – Lastly, the fundamental analysis makes it easier for you to get a grip on the international markets. No matter what country is concerned, you will understand its economy in a glance if you know how to perform fundamental analysis.

The disadvantages are as follows –

- **Overload of Information –** The most obvious disadvantage that you are also going to feel is that fundamental analysis sometimes provides you with so much information that you feel overloaded. In fact, for a beginner, it can be quite overwhelming, and you might even miss out on the important bits amidst such chaos. Thus, the entire process becomes counterproductive.

- **Absence of Market Timing** – When it comes to exits and entries, fundamental analysis cannot really help you – yes, it will give you a broad insight but not such minute technicalities, which are equally important.
  And you must know that timing is the holy grail of trading – you cannot afford to go wrong there. Thus, in order to know when you should enter or exit a particular trade, you have to use technical analysis along with fundamental analysis.

- **Not Meant for the Short Term** – Another grave drawback is that even though you will get the fundamental data of the economy on a monthly basis, it won't really help you in the short-term. There will be a lot of spikes owing to huge volatility.

- **Subjective to a Great Extent** – Yes, there are concrete reasons for everything in fundamental analysis. But an analyst who thinks the price is going to move in a certain way believes so because of a lot of probable reasons, and similarly, an analyst who believes quite the opposite will also give you several believable and concrete reasons.

Technical Analysis

To put it in a gist, we use past movements in price to perform technical analysis. In fact, you will often hear analysts saying that this type of analysis involves less science and more art. Do you know why? It is because sometimes there are nuances occurring in between, mainly because the entire concept of technical analysis relies on predicting price movements based on past data. Thus, sometimes, conclusions might not be the same.

Price data is the first and foremost tool that is used in technical analysis. This is a very important consideration, and it doesn't matter what timeframe you have chosen for this. In fact, you will be provided with a framework through technical analysis that will help you to compare the present data to other historical occurrences of a similar type and study the present price action in detail.

Before we proceed, there are three very important things about technical analysis that you should know –

- Every technical analyst has the belief that the market participants can know everything that there is to know from the current trading price itself. Even if there is some new piece of information, the trading price would quickly reflect it.

- The market always follows certain trends. And if you notice the price changes in a market with a trained eye, you would be able to spot these trends. And these trends are often very much predictable.

- The market has always shown a tendency to repeat history. Thus, trends are of a recursive nature. But I must warn you about something – even though history repeats itself, the trend
might not appear in the exact same way as it did before. There will be some resemblance, but there will also be some newness to it.

Tools

Now let us have a look at some of the common tools used in technical analysis –

- **Forex Volatility Tool** – This tool functions in a specific time period by providing the traders with a pip range. The range of periods could be anything like a week or a day, and the range is the average in that time period. You will be able to set a proper target profit range when you know for certain what the volatility of your currency pair is.

- **Currency Correlation Tool** – Sometimes, there is a relation between the price movements of a currency pair. Suppose a currency pair is moving in the same direction, then the correlation is said to be positive. Similarly, if the currency pair is moving in the opposite direction to each other, then the correlation

21

is said to be negative. When a trader follows a currency table, it becomes easier for them to notice and keep track of such relationships. Knowing these things will help you in better risk assessment and management of the same.

- **Price Action Analysis** – The balance between demand and supply in the market is identified through the price, and so it is a very important tool. In fact, there are traders who trade solely on the basis of price action analysis. They identify the movements in price through the use of candlesticks.

- **Oscillators and Technical Indicators** – This is one of the most popular tools used by technical analysts. There are several types of indicators included under this one, like Bollinger bands, RSI, MACD, Keltner channels, and so on.

Advantages & Disadvantages
Here are some of the advantages of technical analysis –

- **Can Be Done in Any Time Frame –**
  Whether you are trading in the long-term or short-term, technical analysis will be fruitful in all types of time frames.

- **Takes Market Timing Into Consideration** – Unlike fundamental analysis, you can detect your entry and exit from the market with the help of technical analysis. It will tell you when is the best time for executing a particular trade, and everything will be done in an efficient and methodical manner.

- **Helps You Analyze Trends** – Technical analysis uses different types of tools for detecting and studying different market trends. For example,

22

support and resistance, swing highs and lows, moving averages, and so on.

- **Less Overwhelming** – Since there are a lot of things in fundamental analysis, it often gets tiring and overwhelming. But that is not the case with technical analysis because here, everything is a lot more simplified. Price action is the primary variable everywhere in technical analysis, and so things are less complicated.

Now, let us look at some of the disadvantages –

- **Might Give You Mixed Signals** – One of the major drawbacks of technical analysis is that sometimes you might get mixed signals from the different indicators. For example, you might be getting a buy signal from one of the indicators, and at the same time, some other indicator might signal you to sell. This can get you confused and frustrated, and you might end up making the wrong decision.

- **Your Biases Might Influence It** – Technical analysts often get swayed by their biases. For example, if you have a bullish bias, then you might end up overlooking the several signals that point in the opposite direction.
  And the worst part is that you won't even realize that this is happening to you.

- **Chances of Overanalyzing** – Since there are plenty of technical tools that are available to you in today's world, you might end up overanalyzing the situation, and it would only lead to confusion. You won't be able to take a distinct trading decision.

So, I know you might be wondering what to choose – technical analysis or fundamental analysis? Well, it depends entirely on you, but I would suggest you to use a mix of both. But remember that there is no right or wrong answer here. You simply have to use a particular approach and then see whether it works for you or not.

Chapter 3: Basic Forex Trading Strategies That You Should Know

There are countless trading strategies that you can pursue in the world of Forex, but for traders who are just beginning in this world, the most common question is that which strategy should they use? Well, we are going to answer that question in this chapter by providing you with some common and easy strategies. These strategies are the ones you should always keep in your toolbox, and soon, you will realize that they have become a staple in your trading journey.

Once you have mastered these basic strategies, you will become more confident and also become ready to tread onto more advanced grounds.

Breakout Trading

The first strategy that we are going to discuss is something that all of you should learn no matter what. It is also quite easy and simple to grasp, especially for someone who is just starting out. But before we go into the details, I want you to specifically understand what the term 'breakout' means.

In very simpler terms, when there is a movement of price outside of resistance or support areas, then it is termed as a breakout. It is referred to as a bullish breakout when there is an increase in price that goes beyond resistance areas. And then, there are bearish breakout patterns wherein the price decreases below the support areas.

But do you know why this strategy is considered to be so important? Well, the primary reason is that when you identify a point of breakout, it also signifies that the market is going into a very volatile stage. And if you are quick enough, then you can even put this volatility to your advantage by identifying a trend when it begins and joining it.

Your aim should be to enter early and keep riding the trend until there comes the point where the volatility starts to die down. And your stop loss will then have to be placed at a point that is either below or above the breakout candle.

Moving Average Crossover

In this strategy, the average price will be updated constantly so that the price data is smoothed out. The time period of this average can be anything. It can be as much as 30 weeks or 30 minutes – it entirely depends on what you are choosing. The best thing about this strategy is its ability to be tailored to any time frame you want, thus making it appropriate for both short-term and long-term traders.

One of the main reasons why traders prefer this strategy so much is that it helps you in identifying both resistance and support levels. Traders who love to follow technical analysis get the signal when the price of the asset goes beyong the particular moving average.

Now, let us talk about a simple price crossover – among the different trading strategies that involve the moving averages, this is the most common one. When the price of the asset crosses either below or above the moving average, that is when the simple price crossover happens. This means that the trend is about to change.

There is another common strategy used by traders where they implement two moving averages. One moving average is shorter while the other one is longer. A buy signal is generated when the shorter moving average crosses the longer moving average and goes above it. This indicates that the price trend is moving upwards, and so you must sell the asset. This is also known by a popular term – golden cross.

Another variation of the above-mentioned strategy is when it generated a sell signal. It happens when the shorter moving average crosses and goes below the longer moving average. The indication is that the trend in price is moving down. This type of crossover is also referred to by a special name – death cross or dead cross.

Trend Following Strategy

These strategies are perfect for newbies in the forex market. You simply have to observe the market very closely for any changes and patterns. You have to spot a trend assuming that the trend will keep going on in that same direction. There are several reasons why you should be using this strategy. For starters, they are very easy to identify. But before you act on the trend, you need to confirm it. If you think that trading on the trend means that you have to spot when the market is down and buy, and vice-versa then you are wrong. It means that you have to spot the exact time when the market seems to be on the verge of going up, and that is the moment when you need to buy.

Here are some indicators and how they will help you spot these trends emerging

- **Bollinger Bands** – These are most helpful because they assist you in identifying the volatility of the market. You can find out whether the market is in an uptrend or downtrend. You will know that the market is very volatile if the bands are situated at a point that is quite far away from the present trading price. And similarly, it means the opposite when the bands are located very close to the current price. Both these situations should be avoided even more so if you are a beginner. Bollinger bands are mostly used in this way – when the price reaches the upper band, you sell, and when the price reaches the lower band, you buy.

- **Moving Averages** – You already know about moving averages – they help you in finding the direction of the trend. But what you need to keep in mind is that this indicator will not inform you whether the trend is coming to an end or not, and so relying only on them would be a wrong decision. When the present trading price goes below the moving average, you buy, and when it peaks at the moving average or goes above it, you sell.

- **Relative Strength Index (RSI)** – You will understand whether an asset is underbought or overbought with the help of this indicator. An asset is said to be underbought when the RSI is below 30%, and it is said to be overbought when the RSI is above 70%. If there is no change in price and yet the RSI decreases, then you might predict a downtrend. So, before the downtrend actually starts, you need to sell. But relying on RSI cannot be done solely. You have to use other indicators to confirm the signals.

Using Trendlines

This is another simple yet effective strategy that you should learn. You simply have to join two price points (two highs or two lows) on the trading chart with the help of a line. If we assume that there is always some sort of trend in the forex market, then the trendlines will help you identify in which way the trend is moving – is it going up or is it going down? Sometimes we do not recognize certain economic effects or price movements on the charts with our bare eyes, and the trendlines help to identify those.

But if you have been noticing the price to bounce off the same trendline repeatedly, keep in mind that you are not the only one seeing it – others are too. It is true that this type of situation will help you get a few good entries one after the other, but you also have to keep in mind that the trendline won't be there forever. So, before it fails, you need to have your stop loss ready.

There are different tools that are used by traders following the trend trading strategy, and some of them are stochastics, directional indices, volume measurements, RSI, and moving averages. All of these will help you identify and evaluate the trends.

Carry Trade

This is a very specific type of forex trading. When you are dealing with different currencies belonging to different countries, there is often an interest rate difference, and if you can put this difference to your advantage, then that is what carry trade is all about. But at the same time, I'd like to bring to your notice that this type of forex trading can be extremely risky.

However, it is quite popular too.

The basic principle of working of this strategy lies in the fact that the currencies are bought in one day, and then they are held overnight. In this way, the trader gains profit from the interbank interest rate. The catch is to select a country that will give you a lower rate of interest and buy the currency from them so that you can then fund your next purchase – which will be a currency with a higher rate of interest than the previous one. Amazing, isn't it? The difference between these two rates is what will give you the profit. The amount of leverage that you are using will determine how much profit you are making, and mind it; it can be a substantial amount!

Out of all the strategies in the world of forex trading, you will find that this one is quite popular, but as I told you before, it can be quite risky too, and the main reason behind it is that there can be overcrowding because of excess leverage.

But here are some common trading pairs for this strategy – New Zealand dollar/Japanese Yen and Australian dollar/Japanese Yen. These pairs are usually used because the spread of the interest rates in these pairs is quite high and can be used to your advantage.

Momentum Trading

Another very popular strategies used by traders in the forex world is momentum trading. The price trends in recent times are used by traders to buy currencies and then sell them.

Let us say that a trader is implementing the momentum forex trading strategy and if he sees that the price of an asset has started moving in a particular direction; then they make a bet that the direction of movement will remain unchanged.

There are certain aspects of trading that are used to define momentum – for example, the rate of a price change or trading volume. In fact, did you know that research shows, when we are talking about high volumes, there is always that one stock in the market every day that can move up by as much as 30%? This hugely depends on certain announcements and news releases, so you must definitely not miss out on them.

So, the main idea behind momentum trading is that when traders see a strong movement in price in a certain direction, they are of the belief that the price will keep moving in that direction for a certain period of time. Similarly, if you consider the opposite, they like to believe if a movement has weakened, then it means that the trend is most likely to die down. Tools that involve visual analysis like candlestick charts and oscillators are usually used by traders in momentum trading.

Range Trading

Now let us talk about another popular yet very simplified trading strategy of the forex market – range trading. The assumption on which this strategy is based is that prices of currencies when considered within a limited time period, stay within a fixed price range. But this type of trading strategy would be advisable to use only if the economy is predictable and, most importantly, stable. You also have to be sure of the fact that there are no surprise news events coming up that could cause a dent in your plan.

Traders who follow the range trading strategy buy and sell currencies very frequently, and they do so at rates that are highs and lows of resistance and support. In fact, they might even repeat it in a single trading session.

There is a similarity of the tools being used between range traders and trend traders when it comes to fixing an exit and entry point. These include stochastics, commodity channel index, and relative strength index.

Using Purchasing Power Parity Indicator

If you are in search of trading strategies that would be profitable and, at the same time, not too difficult to use for you as a beginner, then using Purchasing Power Parity levels and comparing the exchange rates with them would be a good option.

Now, if you are wondering what the Purchasing Power Parity indicator is, well, it helps you to identify the rate at which the average prices of different services and goods can be equalized. So, you can say that a currency is undervalued if it has been trading at a price that is lower than the PPP. Similarly, a currency is overvalued if its exchange rate is higher than the PPP.

But don't get me wrong. Just because you have decided to follow the PPP indicator for forex trading doesn't mean that the market will do the same at all times. However, if you are considering the major currencies, you will notice that their trading range remains within the 20% range, give or take.

This strategy is very popular among beginners because of its ease of use, but there is something that you should keep in mind – the strategy works best when you are considering trades with a longer time horizon. But if you are considering a shorter time span, for example, a daily basis, you will notice that the exchange rates vary widely, and they keep diverging from the PPP levels by huge numbers. And the balance is not restored any time soon – it can even take weeks for that.

So, now that you have learned about all the major strategies for beginners, the trick to picking the right strategy for yourself lies in choosing the appropriate level of risk management, good money, and leverage. If you do not follow all the basic principles, then no matter how good your strategy is, you will still suffer from huge losses.

If you want to become a professional at forex trading, you have to hone your skills and form good strategies. You also need to have a trading plan about which you will learn in the latter part of this book. Once all of this is in place, you can slowly move on to the more complex strategies. Maintain realistic expectations and enjoy what you are doing.

Chapter 4: Tips For Acquiring the Right Trading Mindset

Developing the right mindset for trading is essential to be successful, but people often fail to realize that. Fear of making mistakes or losing money will be your greatest enemy when it comes to trading, and that fear can be overcome by honing your skills and working on your mindset. Trading psychology is a subject that is widely studied by researchers around the world. It deals with the fact that you need to modify your personality so that you can keep a check on your emotions and not let them mess with your head while you are trading.

Being a successful trader is not only about doing an extensive analysis of market stats or coming up with better strategies; it is also about building the right trading mindset. But most beginner traders believe that only if they can get their hands upon that perfect strategy they can make substantial amounts of profit. But that's not how things work – it's not so easy. If all you needed was a well-formed strategy, then all of us would have been billionaires by now. There are people who have good strategies and yet keep losing huge chunks of money every day.

And there are some traders who have been consistently doing well in the forex market because they have achieved that psychologically right mindset, and that is what differentiates winners from losers.

The world of forex trading needs you to have certain psychological characteristics, attitudes, and beliefs that will help you make more money and be successful in forex trading.

What is a Trading Mindset?

Before I give you some tips on improving your trading mindset, you need to understand what a trading mindset truly is. You have to understand that there is no morality or emotions associated with the market. So, let us say that you want to continue trading in the long run and want to make some substantial profits from it, then you have to form the right mindset for it too, and this can happen once you learn how you can observe the market without being emotionally attached to it.

All your actions ultimately depend on what mindset you carry. You can either make huge profits or suffer huge losses depending on the mindset you have. And even if you do suffer from a loss, the right mindset will prevent you from giving in to the panic and help you make decisions with a sane mind. You cannot afford to base any of your decisions on your emotions, and that is what trading psychology is all about.

A trader who leads a disciplined life will never let anything come in between their trading decisions. But it is not easy to become a disciplined trader, and more importantly, it does not happen overnight. You need to put in an equal amount of effort, willpower, and time and then you can become the disciplined trader you need to be to make successful trades.

Why is it Essential For You to Have a Positive Mindset?

Like you already know – there are no emotions associated with the market – the only emotions at work are those of yours – the market participants. This is also the reason why the different trendfollowing techniques and charting patterns work out brilliantly. They are primarily based on market psychology and human behavior that are predominant.

I don't know whether you have heard of this famous phrase or not, but there is a saying that within 90 days, 90% of the trading funds or 90% of traders will be lost. That means that the successful traders of the market account for only 10%, so what is it that sets them apart? The answer is a positive mindset, and in this chapter, you will learn how you can build one.

There are some traders who are of the belief that the market and everything else is somehow rigged against them – this type of negative mindset hinders their growth. If your thoughts and decisions are clouded by such opinions, then you will never be able to analyze the market from an objective point of view. You have to keep in mind that the market doesn't care whether you win a lot of money or you lose everything – it is completely neutral in that sense.

Thus, if you notice or talk to any of the successful traders or read their interviews, there is one thing that you will find common in every one of them – selfconfidence. They have a belief in their abilities and in themselves, in general – this type of positive mindset and outlook is important. No matter how many trades you lose, this belief should not be shaken.

On the other hand, traders who keep losing all the time often have this looming self-doubt troubling their minds. They think that bad luck follows them all the time or they are cursed or whatever. And with time, this erroneous belief somewhat turns into a self-fulfilling prophecy. When you are not sure about your own decisions or abilities, you will hesitate to take action or initiate trades when you should have, and in this way, you miss out on profit-making opportunities. There is no use in being overly fearful of everything when it comes to trading, and you need to understand this right from the start.

Yes, it is true that sometimes the movements in price cannot be explained by even the best market analysis, but you have to acknowledge and respect that and not blame it on the market being out to get you because there is no such thing as that.

Here Are Some Tips to Groom Your Mindset

A relaxed and calm mindset is what you need to ace at trading. You also need to implement the right risk management strategies, which you will learn in the next chapter. For now, what you need to understand is that even if you lose a trade or two, it's not the end of the world for you. Even the most successful traders in today's world have lost trades, and this happens all the time. Let us say you manage to keep up a winning rate of 50% and your reward-to-risk ratio is set high enough, then you will be able to take home handsome amounts of profit. So, instead of focusing on winning all trades, what you should do is focus on each trade at a time. If you lose, learn from your mistake and try again. If you win, don't consider yourself to be someone who will neve make any mistakes. Stay humble and keep trading.

Also, you need to learn not to take things personally when you are trading. A trade gone bad is just what you see it is – a trade gone bad. There is nothing to be personal about it. The market might not perform in the same way every day, and so, you simply have to implement everything that you have learned and keep faith in the market analysis that you are doing.

So, here are some tips that will help you work on building a trader's mindset and win more trades.

Always Keep Learning

Remember that there is always something new to learn in the world of trading. There are newer strategies, newer modes of analysis, and so on. You need to be a student forever. In fact, one of the most important factors that set a successful trader apart from an unsuccessful one is educating yourself more and more about the trading world and forex markets. This book will help you form a foundation that will get you started, and if you follow everything that I have mentioned here, you will have a comprehensive overview to keep trading.

Education about forex trading is what will help you understand certain market reactions and hence, the price moves. In this way, you will be able to make better predictions. There are endless concepts that you can learn in the world of forex trading. There is literally no end to the list, but what you need to do is figure out which one of these concepts or strategies work the best for you, and then, you need to keep honing your skills and that strategy with time.

There is one thing that you can do to make learning a habit – pick a trading book and promise yourself that you are going to read it at least for an hour before you sleep or any other time of the day when you think you have time. This is a practice that many of the wellknown and successful traders encourage beginners to do. You can also try several trading courses that are now available online.

Never Let Losses Dictate Your Actions

There is a common tendency among beginner traders to let emotions cloud their judgment whenever they lose trades. In fact, there are some traders who believe that they always need to close in a win, and thus, they keep trading and making the wrong decisions even when the market requires them to do the opposite. So, do you see how emotions from losses can hamper your trading career?

You have to learn to cut your losses short. If you see that one of your trades is not performing the way you expected it to, don't wait. Get out of it and minimize your losses. You need to move on to better trades and not keep losing money on the same trade.

Learn to Adjust to the Market

The conditions of the market are not going to be the same at all times. Today the market might be performing well, but in a few weeks, months, or days, it might completely flip from its current position and start going in the opposite direction. You have to be equally flexible and accommodate these changes in your strategy. Maintain your views at a neutral point and then analyze the market. If your analysis says that it is time to change your direction of trading, then you need to do so. Don't let any preconceived notions or emotions overrule your market analysis. Never hesitate to trust your research.

Don't Overwhelm Yourself

There will be times when everything gets messy, and the market is all over the place, and your original strategy no longer holds for the current scenario. Regardless of what is happening around you, you have to maintain an objective outlook. This is what will make you disciplined as a trader. If the market seems to be too chaotic to handle and you think you are not ready for it, don't stress too much and wait for the dust to settle. When you notice a signal that you do recognize, you can then seize the day. Whatever trading strategy or setup you choose to follow, it must have become like a second nature to you by now. If you are planning on taking up a new setup, then practice it in market conditions that you are habituated in. Once you have become a master in that trading setup, only then use it in crisis situations.

Be Persistent

Lastly, I'd like to remind you that no one became a successful trader overnight. It takes time, patience, and experience to become an expert at something. Just because you faced a few losses doesn't mean that you will quit and leave. Take it as a learning experience – let your mistakes teach you something.

Keep a journal where you will note down all your trades, for example, your entry and exit points or why you chose to enter that trade in the first place. You can also jot down some additional comments that you want your future self to remember.

You will identify a lot of trading patterns from your journey by maintaining a trading journal. It will help you improve your skills.

So, now that you have read the chapter, I want to remind you that if you seriously want to be a successful trader, you cannot sit on your couch and procrastinate. You have to get up and put in some actual effort. As we all know that every trade comes with its share of risks, and risk management is an equally important part of being a successful trader, which is what brings us to our next chapter.

Chapter 5: Money and Risk Management to Avoid Losses

In this chapter, I am going to give you a crash course on how you can minimize your losses and maximize your profits in forex trading through the right strategies of money and risk management. Many beginners think that if they have figured out the direction of price movement in the forex market, then they have won the trade, but that's only one side of the coin. The other side comprises risk management. Trading in the forex market always has a lot of risks, and if you cannot take steps to manage that risk, you are going to lose money one way or the other.

Traders, especially the newbies, have the habit of neglecting this aspect of trading; however, it is not a clever thing to do. But if you want to become successful in trading, there are a few risk management rules that you have to keep in mind, and we are going to learn those rules in detail in this chapter.

Before we move on to the rules, I want to introduce you to the common types of risk that you will be dealing with in the forex market.

- **Interest Rate Risk** – This is also the risk that is a result of volatility. Volatility in the market is what leads to abrupt changes in interest rates. When you consider the whole economy, there is a change in the amount of investment and spending, which changes the foreign exchange rates.

- **Currency Risk** – Then we come to the currency risk whereby the prices of currencies undergo a fluctuation causing the currencies to become less or more expensive when it comes to purchasing foreign assets.

- **Leverage Risk** – This applies to those traders who are trading on a margin because they stand a chance of experiencing losses that are hugely magnified. The value of the forex trade, in this case, is much bigger than the initial outlay, and so, beginner traders often forget how much amount they are leaving at risk.

- **Liquidity Risk** – This is when you want to prevent a loss, but you cannot do so because you cannot sell or purchase the currency as quickly as you need to. Yes, I know that I have told you at the beginning of this book that one of the advantages of forex trading is its high liquidity, but there might be certain scenarios when there is illiquidity. This mostly happens because of the release of certain government policies that suddenly changes the playing ground for everyone.

Trade With Capital That You Can Afford to Lose

The first and foremost tip for managing your money and limiting your risk is to trade only with that amount of money that you can afford to lose. It's quite simple, really. You need to deposit a certain amount of money to your trading account, right? So, this amount should not be more than what you can afford.

To make the process easier, evaluate the expenditures that you have every month. And then, think about it long and hard and then set a particular value that is acceptable to lose for you in a month. You have to make a note of the fact that if you have already touched this level, then you need to stop trading at all costs. The main aim of this tip is that you should not be risking an amount of money that could drastically turn your life upside down if you happen to lose it. Thus, a rule of thumb is not to put your money for essential needs into trading. This includes the money you need every month to pay for your mortgage, rent, commutes, food, other bills, and so on. Remember that even though trading can earn you quite a fortune, it's not a guaranteed money-making machine. So, you will be making a lot of mistakes and lose some money before you learn to trade successfully. Thus, don't lose any money that you cannot afford to part with.

Don't Chase the Market

Now, let us discuss the next most important thing in forex trading – you have to resist the urge to chase the market. When someone is new in the world of forex trading, they do not understand the risks associated with chasing each and every trading opportunity. Some of them might not have sufficient chances of winning, and when you chase such a trade setup, there are high chances that you will end up with a big loss. Newbies are often excited to have their new trading account, and being in the forex market that they overlook other important factors. They even place more than one trades within an hour just because they think one of them is bound to bring them profit, but things don't work that way. If someone exercises this type of behavior, then it is more like gambling and less trading.

You have to keep it in your mind that there is nothing that is owed by the market to you. In order to be a successful trader, you need to have a lot of patience, and with time, you will understand that even more. For example, if, on a particular day, you do not find sufficient solid trading opportunities, you need to take a step back and wait for your entry the next day. Chasing the market will not bring you anything. No matter how much profit you have made, never forget that a single losing trade is enough to take away everything you won.

Learn to Quantify the Money You Are Risking in Each Trade

In the first point, I already explained that you should not be trading with the money that you need for your day-to-day essentials. So, once you have figured out the amount of money that you are going to put into your trades, it is time that you also figure out the sum that you are risking in each trade. But why do you need this? Well, figuring out the risking value will help you set the stop loss. Quantifying your risk can be easily done, and there are two methods from which you can choose –

- **A Fixed Percentage** – The first method is the most common one whereby you maintain a fixed percentage of your trading account balance that you are going to risk in every trade. So, let us assume that the balance in your trading account is $10,000, and you have decided to quantify your risks at 2%, then every trade that you make will be risking an amount of $200. So, what is the advantage of using this process? It will ensure that even if you lose a trade, the whole account balance is not lost. Moreover, the higher the amount of trading capital you possess, the higher you can risk in any trade because you have set it at 2%. But there is also a disadvantage to this method. If someone has suffered a setback of losses

45

one after the other, then there will come the point where their account balance has diminished a lot, and the amount of money they have left or
they are risking is very low. The direct result of this is that winning back the money you lost will also take you quite some time.

- **A Fixed Sum** – Another school of thought is that you should set your risk limit per trade at a fixed amount rather than a fixed percentage. For example, a trader might decide to risk $500 in every trade when they have deposited an amount of $10,000 in their trading account. The rule is not too hard to keep in mind or follow. The advantage is that you know exactly how much amount of money is at risk for each trade. So, if you decide to make a total of five trades a day, no matter what, the total amount of money you stand to lose is $2,500 and not more than that. But the disadvantage with this system is that you risk $500 in every trade irrespective of how much you have in your trading account. At the same time, if your trading account balance has increased to a great extent owing to some consecutive wins, you will not be risking much and thus, miss out on greater returns just because you thought of risking only $500 in every trade. On the contrary, if you have lost a maximum portion of your money and you have only $2,000 in your account, in that case, risking $500 in every trade means risking a substantial portion of your total trading account.

Design a Good Trading Plan

You can make your forex trading experience way easier only if you have a well-designed trading plan with you. It will act as a guide to help you make decisions while trading. In fact, if the market becomes volatile, making the right decisions at the right time can be tricky, but a good trading plan can make it easier and also encourage discipline. If your trading plan is built the right way, then it should answer your questions of when, what, how much, and why you are trading.

Every trading plan is different. The main idea behind building trading plans is that they should be made somehow personal to you, having your own ideas and your personal touch. If you want to just copy someone else's trading plan, it will not help you in any way. The main reason behind this is that the person whom you are copying might not have the same goals as you. Their ideas and attitudes might not match yours, and so, their trading plan is not going to work for you. Another significant difference between your trading plan and that of others is the amount of money you are ready to risk in trading – it might not be the same as that of the other person.

Lastly, I'd like to remind you of the importance of maintaining a trading journal or a diary – this will help you keep a record of all the trades that you are placing and all strategies that you are implementing. You should even note down your emotional state during each trade. We will cover the topic of building a trading plan in detail in the next chapter.

Cut Your Losses Short

A rule of thumb followed in all forms of trading – be it forex trading or any other type of trading – is that you have to cut your losses short. In simpler terms, if you notice that one of your trades is not performing well and things have not panned out the way you thought they would, then the losses from your trade will keep accumulating. In that case, you have to close the trade as soon as you can. Similarly, when your trade is performing well, you need to keep it running but only up to a certain point. You need to fix a stop loss and not be too greedy – you never know when everything changes. Stay aware of the conditions of the market so that you can get out of the trade at the right time and bring home huge profits.

Traders who have just begun often don't follow this rule. When they start losing money in a trade, they think that keeping it open is the best thing to do so that they can wait for the course to eventually run in the opposite direction. Similarly, they sometimes exit out of profitable trades too soon because they fear losing out on money. Greed and fear are two of the most dangerous emotions to fester in the world of trading. If you want your trading career to grow, you need to let go of these emotions.

Set a Risk-Reward Ratio

In the previous steps, you have learned that you need to set a fixed amount of money that you are willing to risk in each trade. Once that is done, the next step is to figure out how much profit you are aiming to make in the next trade. That level will mark the take profit level for each trade.

Your aim of profit will largely depend on your profile of trading and the strategies that you use. And most importantly, it is your risk appetite that will determine your profit-taking mark.

Now, let us assume that you have set your risk to reward ratio at 1:1 then; that would mean, if your acceptable amount of loss is $200, then your profit target in that trade should also be $200. However, for someone who has a risk to reward ratio of, say 1:3, then they would have a target profit f $600 with the same acceptable amount of $200 as a loss.

The general rule of thumb in forex trading is that your ratio of risk to reward should be something that is greater than 1:1. Do you know why? This is because even if you lose two trades in a row and then win two trades in a row, you would have a net profit, but if the ratio was 1:1, then, in this case, your net profit would have been $0.

Use Limits and Stops

As you must have already understood by now, volatility is a common presence in the forex market. So, even before you open a new position during your trade, you need to have your exit points ready. There are different types of limits and stops that will help you out regarding this –

- **Guaranteed Stops** – These stops will ensure that you exit from the trade at the specific price that you have stated. In this case, the risk of slippage can be avoided.

- **Normal Stops** – Then there are normal stops – their main function is to find their position on their own the moment the market starts going in the opposite direction. But protection from slippage is not guaranteed here.

- **Trailing Stops** – The nature of these stops is such that they closely follow the positive movements in price, and whenever there is a move that works against you, the trailing stop will exit your position in the trade.

- **Limit Orders** – Here, the main aim is to set a take-profit level and then follow it. Once the profit has hit that level, your position will be closed.

Be Careful About Leverage

Using too much leverage during trading is one of the most common mistakes, especially among beginners. You need to understand that even though leverage allows you to trade more, it is essentially a doubleedged sword. It is true that you will be able to increase your profits by ten folds because of leverage, but it is also true that if things don't work out the way you wanted them to, then it is the same leverage that will cause you to lose ten times more money. Trading on leverage is the most tempting thing to do in the world of forex trading because it will allow you to keep increasing the volume of your trading account. But, at its core, this is not how you should be trading.

The first thing to keep in mind as a trader is that you have to protect your capital. Always keep the downside of trade in mind when you open a position and before you think about your potential profit, think about your potential loss. To determine what your appropriate amount of leverage should be, there are several things that you should consider, for example, the size of your trading account, the stop-loss distance, and the risk-per-trade that you have determined.

Don't Forget Currency Correlations

We know that in the forex market, currencies are taken in pairs, and they are priced in that same manner. So, in order to become a successful trader in the forex world, you need to understand the correlation between these currencies.

In this way, you will be able to build a better Forex portfolio, and your overall risks are also reduced. Everything will remain in your control. But what does correlation mean? It means studying the changes in one currency that are caused by the change of price of the currency in the pair. The currencies will move in the same direction if there is a positive correlation between them. Similarly, they will move in the opposite direction if there is a negative correlation between them.

Keep Emotions in Check

In trading, beginners often let their emotions come in between their trading decisions, and that is something you cannot afford to do. Your emotions will be triggered by the high amount of volatility in the forex market, but you cannot let yourself get overwhelmed. Emotions like doubt, temptation, greed, fear, and anxiety will not allow you to see things from an objective point of view, and you will simply start thinking from your heart. But letting your emotions get the better of you will only affect your trade outcome negatively.

So, if you are just starting out, all the money and risk management tips that I have mentioned in this chapter should help you find the right path. Once you have made your trading decisions, it is also important for you to stick to them no matter what. And like anything else in the world, being better at trading needs more and more practice. You can start with a demo account if you are a complete newbie.

With a demo account, you can test your strategies and make mistakes without worrying about the risks involved. Demo accounts will give you the chance to trade with virtual funds rather than risk your actual capital and lose your money. In this way, you will slowly get a better grasp of things and understand how the forex market works. You can also back-test your strategies and your trading plan with your demo account and then figure out all those places where there is room for improvement.

It is okay to make mistakes, but it is also important that you learn from them and promise yourself not to make the same mistakes again. If you suffer losses, learn to take responsibility for them. Don't play the blame game and blame the market for your loss – you need to understand that it is only you who determines what happens to the money in your trading account.

Chapter 6: How to Create a Trading Plan?

What we mean by a trading plan is nothing else by kind of a guide, or a sort of a map to help the investor to take proper decisions regarding this trade and to highlight to him what are the risks, what are the profit points and to help him draw out a plan so that his business runs smoothly. A proper trading plan should ideally tell an investor what his objectives should be to reach that goal, what are the risks he might have to face, how much time will he need to get there. An ideal trading plan should technically also point out the most profitable entry and exit points for the investor and the correct position sizing rules.

The plan should ideally also point out the position sizing rules, risk management techniques, how he will find the trade, and how he will need to execute them in return. The correct time and conditions under which the investor can buy or sell securities and, most importantly what are the kinds of securities that need to be purchased in the first place should also be indicated by the plan. The kind of securities that should be dealt with and the nature and position of their management are also important information that should be provided by the trading plan.

Along with these, a trading plan, which is basically a management guide, should guide you as to how to develop a proper trading system. It is ultimately a well-drafted trading plan that will help the investor to work in the market with minimum problems, and thus, quite naturally, it needs to be well researched and well-drafted, and it should also ideally provide the investor with adequate space for making any changes or adjustments later so that any kind of emergencies can be met at short notice. Every investor is supposed to have some personal preferences, objectives, and his/her unique way of going about their work in the market. And hence, it is the trading plan that tells us about their unique approach and style which sets them apart from other investors out there.

An indispensable part of any financial transaction, a trading plan is something that is highly recommended by every expert to their next in lines as any serious investment is bound to be backed by a well made and well-thought trading plan. For everyone who is newly exploring this field should know from the very beginning that it is of utmost importance to create down a detailed trading plan at the onset of starting an investing plan. Those who are veterans in this field will already know that your trading plan should ideally have a summary of all the key points regarding every step you are going to take so that you can have a clear picture of what you are getting yourself into. Having a solid idea of what are the strategies you want to take will keep you ready for everything that is to come. So, all in all, your trading plan will make the entire process of forex trading much easier for you and will definitely make it a much more convenient initiative to take.

What is the Need for a Trading Plan?

Having a trading point is of utmost importance as it helps you to actually take the journey from theory to experience. From reading and learning about the entire trading and investment plan to actually practicing it in the real market, it is ultimately the trading plan that helps you actualize it. Doing anything without proper knowledge of it will only lead to numerous problems and impending disasters. But having prior knowledge about it makes it easier. No matter how much you read about trading and marketing, it will never give you your needed expertise. It's like learning driving, and getting a license is not enough. Unless you actually drive that car by yourself, on a busy road, you will never gain confidence. Similarly, unless you actually draw up a plan and start taking action, you will not gain enough experience to make any difference. Only by maintaining a proper plan will you get to know about your own limitations and strengths, and that will, in turn, help you take sensible actions.

Steps to Create a Successful Trading Plan

Till now, we discussed what a trading plan is and why it is so very important to have a detailed trading plan before you start forex trading. Now that we have successfully established the importance of having a plan let us now discuss how to actually formulate a plan in real life. We understand that at times it might be a little too daunting but fear not. We have you covered. Down below, I am listing some easy, comprehensible steps to make a trading list that will help you understand the process with much ease so that you can develop your skills further.

- **Understand your skills -** This step is primarily for you. It's about you to ask yourself whether you want to actually trade or not. Then go ahead to ask yourself what kind of trading you want to go forward with. What are the risks you are comfortable in taking, what you think your strengths are, and how much do you think you can deal with? After you get these answers from yourself, you are ready for further planning.

- **Preparing yourself -** After you have your thoughts clear regarding your wants and expectations, it is highly important to prepare yourself both physically

55

and mentally for what is to come. It is highly advisable not to neglect any physical needs like proper food and rest prior to the day of trading, as you will need all your strength. Simultaneously, if there is anything disturbing you mentally, it is advisable to deal with it before so that you have nothing to distract you on that day.

- **Fix your goals** - Both for beginners as well as for those with experience, it is very important to have a clear picture of your risk/reward
ratio. You should have a practical idea regarding what your goals are. If you start with extremely ambitious goals, it might so be that you find it extremely hard to reach that goal for the first time. What will happen as a result is that you might get demotivated to take further actions. But this shouldn't be the situation ideally. So, in the beginning, it will always be advisable to wrap your head around the actual practical picture and set yourself goals that you will not have much difficulty in reaching. Once you know what you want, it will be much easier to work accordingly so as to get that.

- **Set an upper limit for your risk level** - It is necessary for you to understand that no matter how much invested you are mentally with a certain trade, if you can estimate that it is going up above the risk limits you can handle, then you need to reform your strategies or in extreme cases, change your plans altogether. You simply can't let yourself go beyond a certain risk level. So, set yourself a limit. Anywhere between 1% to 5% is all right. If whatever trade you have taken up remains within this limit, it means that you can rearrange your strategies if any emergency. Anything beyond that means you need to rethink the trade before going ahead with it.

- **Do your homework well** - Before you start
with anything, it is absolutely necessary to do a thorough background check on everything that is related to your project. Get to know whether the currencies you want are up or down, do your research well both for your domestic and international market. Don't forget to run a check on all the data regarding economic policies. This is one of the most important parts of your entire trading process, as a huge chunk of your trading policies will depend on these market analysis and data, so you absolutely need to get these correct.

- **Prepare your trade well** - You need to select a method that suits you best in order to keep track of your trade journals. Once you have decided how to keep track of your trade, you now need to label what you think are the minor and major resistance and the support levels. After that, set yourself a convenient alert for all your entry and exit points.

- **Set the rules for entry and exit** - Both entry and exit points are of prime importance in any trade, so you really can't prioritize one over the other. Plan them ahead so that no problems arise later. You need to analyze your profit targets and breakeven points for setting the rules of your entry and exit points. What this will do is also help you by giving you an additional option B, in case things go wrong with your option A.

- **Maintain your records properly** - After you have collected all your data, your task is to maintain that and keep that updated. Mark out what your long-term and short-term strategies are. This will be your guidebook for handling any situation.

- **Analyze your performance** - Your trading

plan will be your best critique as it will give you a clear picture of all your past and present trading actions, giving you a clear picture regarding how your future trades should be. It will make you learn from your mistakes and help you increase your future profit margins.

Conclusion

Thank you for making it through to the end of *Forex for Beginners*; let's hope it was informative and able to provide you with all of the tools you need to achieve your goals, whatever they may be.

There are so many people who start trading in the forex market each and every day. It's not difficult to start. All you have to do is do some research and take the first step. And if you have reached this page in the book, then you are ready to take that first step. With the boom of the internet, forex trading is no longer complicated. In fact, it has become more accessible and convenient. Forex trading has been growing significantly over the past few years, and now, it is time that you put your skills to good use and make money.

But I'd strictly advise you to first make a plan. Don't jump in right away. Make a plan and stick to it no matter what. In trading, the slow and steady wins the race. As you keep placing each trade, you will learn something new about the market. With time, these lessons will give you more success. Make the best use of a demo account because it will help you practice trading in an environment that mimics the market and yet is risk-free, which, in simpler terms, means that you are not losing any money here.

Finally, if you found this book useful in any way, a review on Amazon is always appreciate!